My Child...
God Speaks to His Children

Jennifer Turner

David Turner International Ministries
www.DTIM.org

My Child...
God Speaks to His Children

Copyright © 2023 Jennifer Turner
First Printing

All rights reserved. No part of this publication may be reproduced, stored in a retrieval, or transmitted in any form or by any means, electronic, mechanical, photocopy, recording, or otherwise, without the permission of the publisher or in accordance with the provisions of the Copyright, Designs, and Patents Act of 1988 or under the terms of any license permitting limited copying issued by the Copyright Licensing Agency.

Scripture taken from the New King James Version® Copyright 1982 by Thomas Nelson, Inc. Used by permission. All rights reserved.
The emphasis in scripture quotations is from the author.

Special thanks and acknowledgment:
Cover Art by Julia Rose © Believer Christian Art.
Editorial, layout, and book design - Lin Marie Carey.
Photography - Rick Sanchez © Rick Sanchez Photography.

A publication of David Turner International Ministries
www.DTIM.org

ISBN: 979-8-218-28811-2

Published in the United States of America

Dedication

I dedicate this book to God Jehovah, God Jesus Christ, and God Holy Spirit. Everything I am and everything that I have is from Your hand. My heart's desire is to accomplish exactly what You have dreamed and ordained for my life. I cherish the spiritual gifts you have given me, and I am thankful for the passion you poured upon my heart to pray in the Spirit.

To my spiritual father, Harry Gomes...
When I met you, I Samuel 18:1 became a living word for me. Just as the souls of Jonathan and David were knit together, my soul was knit with yours. It was a divine relationship ordained by God. I knew you were a man of God from the moment I heard you preach, and I feel blessed and privileged that the Lord would bring you into my life in such a beautiful way.

To my husband, David...
You are a man after God's heart and an inspiration to my life. Serving the Lord alongside you has been the adventure of a lifetime. Thank you for your love, care, guidance, and support.

To my son, Christopher, and his darling wife Rachel...
God has made me a mother to many, and you have been the training ground. The hand of the Lord is upon you as you walk this wonderful journey together. You bring unspeakable joy to my life.

A Special Message

from the Author, Jennifer Turner.

My Child...

God Speaks to His Children

Jennifer Turner

Day 1

My Child...

Rise up, beloved.
Shake off the dust and ash...fire of God, fire from the altar.
My eyes are looking to and fro throughout the earth so I can strengthen the hearts of those completely loyal to Me.
Be willing to be set apart for Me and My purposes.

It may be a season in the desert,
However, you must be saturated and soaked in Me just as the dew of Hermon descends upon the mountains of Zion.
It is there I have commanded the blessings...
showers of blessings all around you.

You must decrease for Me to increase, beloved.
You are united with Jesus Christ, the Messiah.
As Abraham's child, you inherit all the promises of
My Kingdom realm. Be a good receiver...
receive all you need from Me, for I give it all to you.

Day 2

My Child...

Trust in Me with everything, not in your own wisdom or understanding. When you honor Me with your very best, and with your increase, every dimension of your life will overflow with blessing from an uncontrollable source of inner joy.

My eye is upon you.
I hear you and will answer you before you even call to Me.
While you are still speaking, I hear you. (Isaiah 65:24)
I will answer you. I am willing and able to do all things.
Surrender and walk with Me.
I must increase and you must decrease.
To die is gain. When you decrease, you can take ground.

Day 3

My Child...

My beloved, be willing to lose yourself for My sake.
Let your heart not be troubled...
or your mind race with thoughts on how, when, or why.
Fix your heart on My heart for you.
Be swept away...swept off your feet by My great love for you.
When your heart is consumed with Me, on fire for Me,
there will be no limits to what you can do if you are all in with Me.

By our agreement, we can touch a generation when you
join your spirit with Mine. Let that thought stir your heart.
Let Me go before you and be the breaker that breaks down every
wall, door, and limitation.
You can let Me do it or you can do it for yourself...
but the time is short.
I have given you free will to occupy your heart and mind
with whatever you desire.

I desire that you trust Me completely...
give Me every worry, anxiety, doubt, and fear.
You will be free when you surrender it to Me...
free to walk with Me and hear My voice without interruption.

Day 4

My Child...

You are Mine.
I am delighted by your lovely worship and pure heart of devotion.
There is always a way with Me.
You are never at a dead end or without.
I part the seas. My voice splinters the mighty trees of Lebanon.
I command the angel armies.

Natural laws do not limit Me. I expand and spread.
I am omnipresent, omnipotent. I create omni signs and wonders.
I love to do small things that bless you daily just to hear you say, *"Thank you, daddy."* I am smiling over you when you acknowledge Me every day. I shower you with blessings as a token of My great love and affection for you.

I am singing My Songs of love and deliverance over you.
You have allowed many things to be built around you for protection. These things keep you from receiving the fullness of My love...the deep revelation of My love for you.
I saw those that hurt you and did not love you
as they should have. That changed you.
Allow My Spirit to wash you.
Healing is here, beloved. Healing is your birthright.
Your identity and worth can only be found in Me.

I release My joy upon you.
Allow it to overtake you and receive hope.
All things are found in Me...
you will find your way through Me.

Day 5

My Child...

You are complete by your union with Jesus Christ.
He is head over every ruler and authority.
He took everything against you and put it on the cross.
He disarmed the spiritual rulers and authorities. He shamed them publicly and made a spectacle of them. He has given you power over them...to disarm...and put them under your feet.

Therefore, be strong and courageous in the power of His might.
Have no fear...
you have a cloud of heavenly witnesses around you.
What is pulling at you in this realm can feel much more powerful than My Kingdom, but don't fall into that trap.
You have the whole Kingdom of Heaven behind you and all around you. There are more with you than with them.
Keep your eyes on things above.
My Son is interceding for you at My throne.
All things are available to you and for you.
You are not "less than."

You are elevated to do the good works I have prepared for you.
I brought you into this world for My good pleasure.
Find your place in Me...
find rest in Me and do all things from that resting posture.
My Kingdom does not operate in frustration, worry, or anxiety, which are fruits of the enemy. He has been disarmed.
He only has what you give him and what you allow.

Be aware...look for the territory you have given him from your life, your ground. It is the place you have given him to stand and drip poison to you...death.
Root it out. Take back the ground.
That is what was bought for you at such a high price.
Don't live below.
Live above, seated with Me.

Day 6

My Child...

My beloved, wherever you are in your walk with Me, I want to take you to the next level until you swim in the knowledge of Me.
From your toes to your ankles and your shins to your knees, be submerged...soak in Me.
Let the things of this world with a place in your heart become secondary to Me. There will be a peace that takes over the atmosphere when I become your complete joy...a peace that will be present and above all the worldly pulls and noise.
Then, that which I have placed on you and in you will grow.

What you have overcome will become a cornerstone in your life, enabling you to set others free.
You will bring healing words of encouragement.
We will walk together and change the atmosphere
for My Kingdom and glory. Swim in Me.
These are the dominion and domain I want you to understand.
They are here and available for you.

Day 7

My Child...

There are many characteristics to your nature by My design.
You are a child. You are the one I can command and direct.
You are a warrior.
You are a spirit walking in a natural, fleshly realm.
You are a sharpener to others.
You are a comforter.

My righteous ones are bold as lions...
and they don't shrink back in any situation.
What you need in any moment I will provide.
I supply grace for you that is over, around, covering, smearing,
and spreading. Put your hand to the plow and don't look back.
Work in My Vineyard. Eat, enjoy, laugh, and love greatly.
Grace, grace, grace.

As you die daily, crucifying your flesh,
you are made alive and new in Me.
You have new depths, heights, and widths.
You have all eternity, and you have My permission
to explore how far you can go in My Spirit.
It is endless, beloved, it is endless!
Don't grow weary in temporal pain and problems,
for they do not compare to the light of eternity.
Encourage yourself in Me.

Speak to your soul.
Arise and shine for the Light of the World has dawned upon you.
The living water is pouring forth from your bellies,
able to bring the dead things back to life.
There is a newness that is available to you.
You can wake up in this newness each day.
Wake up to a new level in Me and see yourself in Me...
endless, boundless, full, healed, and whole.
Lacking nothing...lacking nothing.

...continued.

Let the truth of lacking nothing penetrate your depths...
meditate upon this truth.
Eat that truth and let it become the reality you walk in
and wake up to daily.
You lack nothing in love, peace, joy, or kindness.
You lack nothing in self-control.
You lack nothing in long-suffering.
There may just be unsubmitted areas in your life that need to come
under My blood...submitted and crucified.
It's up to you how deep and wide you are willing to go and give.
Choose this day how far you will go with Me.

Day 8

My Child...

My grace is sufficient for you.

(This is a response of a yielded heart to the Father...)
To behold your beauty, Father, is my undoing.
One glimpse of your splendor and this world fades away.
Who can stand in your glorious presence?
Who am I to ask, *"Why have you created Me this way?"*
I am here for your pleasure and your purposes.
I am your workmanship, created in Christ Jesus,
to walk in the good works prepared for me.

I am yours, for your possession, that I may proclaim the
excellencies of Jesus, the One who called me from darkness into
His marvelous light. Make me your mouthpiece to proclaim.
Touch my lips with the holy fire. Purify my speech.
Joy overtakes me as I think about your faithfulness
and your goodness to me.

Day 9

My Child...

You will taste the abundant life when you allow the Holy Spirit to put to death the corrupt ways of the flesh.
Do not get discouraged when you face trials of many kinds.
I am with you.
When you do not see a solution or a way out,
surrender it all to Me and I will be the light to your path
that makes a way. There is never a dead end for Me.
There is never a situation I cannot handle.
I have not forgotten you.
I know where you are always and what you are facing.

Guard your heart and mouth.
Speak in alignment with My Word.
This life and the things you are going through are temporal.
If they entangle and derail you,
you are no longer running your race.
Keep your eyes on things above.
Examine yourself.
Be aware of the traps of the enemy...
the buttons he pushes over and over again.
It is time to overcome.
There is grace for you to go to the next level.
Put your hand to the plow, and don't look back.

The time is now.
Be ready to hear and obey.
My eyes are looking throughout the whole earth
to see whose hearts are loyal unto Me,
that I may show Myself strong on their behalf.

Day 10

My Child...

You are worried about many things,
but only one thing is needed...love.
It is vital you understand how greatly and perfectly you are loved.
You have two divine intercessors praying for you each day...
the Holy Spirit and Jesus Christ.
Love has conquered and made you a conqueror.
Remain steadfast...learn to rest in Me, and the victory will come.
It is not by your will or by running here and there. (Romans 9:16)
It is not by your strength or might but by My Spirit. (Zechariah 4:6)

Come, have fellowship with Me.
Come and drink deeply of the living water.
My spirit is more than enough for this world, beloved.
I am calling My obedient warriors to the forefront.
I provide a broad path for your feet. (Psalm 18:36)
I am a shield for you.
You will pursue My enemies and overtake them.
Do not turn back until they are destroyed.
They will all lose heart and come trembling from their strongholds.
I arm you with strength for the battle.

The kingdom comes through My children.
My eyes are looking throughout the whole earth for those who are faithful to Me and who count the cost and say, *"I will go."*
Those who say, *"I am here, send Me."* are My sent ones.
Give Me your heart and your devotion of love.
Separate yourselves from the things of this world.
Come out from among the worldly people and be separate.

Day 11

My Child...

I created the heavens and the earth.
I created your innermost being. You are My handiwork.
I am the builder of everything.
I make everything beautiful in its time.
You know in part and prophesy in part.
Come to Me. I bring clarity and give you wisdom by My Spirit.
Confusion is not in My presence. Ask the Holy Spirit to help you.
Ask Him to give you the words to speak.
Ask Him to put My Word in you and it will bring forth
a wellspring of life and salvation.
The Word will become supernatural, taking root, and giving life.

Encourage yourself in My Word. Wear it as truth armor.
The lies can't pierce this armor if you believe My Word.
I held nothing back from My creation, My family.
I gave all. I am for you, and I am with you.
My righteous ones are bold as lions.
Do not fear, I am for you. I pierce you.
I heal you...you are a new creation. All creation waits in eager
expectation for Me to show who My children are.
I will show myself strong on your behalf.
Don't be afraid to open your mouth wide, for I will fill it.

Day 12

My Child...

My beloved, there is no lack when you are in Me.
No good thing do I withhold from those who
walk uprightly before Me. (Psalm 84:11)
Where there is lack or a place the enemy has stolen from you,
simply trust Me...allow Me to fill that space
and grow you to a new level.
Many worldly things try to fill those voids, beloved.
But look to Me...I will order your steps and keep your feet
steady and on My path of life.

Don't hold any expectation of how or what I will give you in place
of those worldly things. Meditate on My great love for you.
My love...My goodness...My faithfulness...My joy...My generosity.
I have always given you My very best. I gave you My Son.
What else would I give you? Everything...the best of everything.

Change your mindset to match Mine for you.
You must become a good receiver.
I am a giving God who loves to give lavishly.
Receive all the good I have for you, beloved.
It is My joy to see you blessed, complete, and overflowing.
Your valley of tears has ended. Your season of overflow is here.
No more will the enemy have his way in your life.

What I need you to accomplish requires you to be overflowing.
It is your inheritance, your right as My child.
Receive...open your mouth wide and I will fill it.
You are My watchman on the wall.
You are My warrior.

Day 13

My Child...

As you draw near to Me and seek Me, I will be found.
I am a rewarder.
Put Me first and cast all your cares upon Me,
for I care deeply for you.
I am everywhere.
Open your eyes to see My beauty all around you in the everyday things. I send sweet things daily.
See them and acknowledge Me in them.
Your joy will begin to multiply.
I want to give you your heart's desire for My glory.

I delight in you, My child.
I have given you all things.
You have not because you ask not.
Ministering spirits are here for you.
My strength is here for you. Ask Me for anything.
I desire for you to feel no lack, no lack.

Overflow in Me, overflow in Me, overflow in Me.
Rivers of living water are flowing in you.
I want you to look with spiritual eyes and spiritual understanding rather than natural eyes and natural understanding.

Day 14

My Child...

Wildest dreams...wildest dreams.
I will do more than you can ask, think, or imagine. (Ephesians 3:20)
Dream about how intimate and far-reaching My love is for you.
My mighty power will work in you to accomplish all things.
I will achieve infinitely more than your request,
your most unbelievable dream.
I will exceed your wildest imagination.
I will outdo them all,
for My miraculous power constantly energizes you, My beloved.
If I say it, beloved, trust it. If I say it, be obedient to it.

The world is hurtful, wounding, and hardening.
I need you soft and gentle, perfected, in love.
Be bathed in My perfect love for you, which expels all fear.
Accept what I have said as the only truth.
Put away all the lies the enemy has put on you.
Feel the weight of My glory.
Let Me wrap you in it and fill you with love and security.
Be lost in Me. Lose yourself in Me.

My bride, you are being prepared without spot or wrinkle.
I see you as I created you. I am delighted with you.
I want all of you. I am jealous for you.
To dream wildly you must have the revelation of your worth and understand the depth of My love for you.
Dive in. You have yet to scratch the surface.
It is deep and wide and far.

You can walk easily through trials and tribulations.
You can laugh and be light, filled with joy.
It is a choice because I am with you.
My presence gives you that option, so choose well.
Choose to lose yourself in Me.

Day 15

My Child...

I am on My throne.
My Kingdom will have no end.
I am eternity and have no limitations.
No one is limiting you, My child.

I know there are things you want changed.
Be patient and look to Me. Change will come.
Trust in Me...rest in Me.
There is not a single thing we cannot overcome together.
All things are possible when we walk in tandem and unity...
when we are yoked together.
With man, it is impossible. Why? Because the flesh is weak.
With Me, all things are possible to him who is willing to believe.

I have such a high calling on your life.
Be a lover of Me, for I love My people.
Love is My high calling for you.
Let Me love you and fill you to overflowing.
Be a good receiver. Receive My love and receive My joy.

Day 16

(From the author: I had a vision of a branch grafted onto the vine as a baby in its mother's womb, connected by the umbilical cord. The baby is receiving nourishment and growth through that connection alone.)

My Child...

I am the vine, and you are grafted in as a branch.
As you rest in Me, stay in Me.
You will grow in your spiritual authority,
and when we walk into a room together,
we will change the atmosphere.
Together, we will bring change.

Move with Me. Ask Me for direction.
You will hear Me give it to you.
I will say when, where, go, stop.
We walk together in unity...not in legalism, but in love.
Do not go in your power, strength, or wisdom, and then ask Me to bless what you have done. I want our union to be so close that we can move together to take ground for My Kingdom.
I release the bands of the enemy off you, My child.

Day 17

My Child...

Give Me your first fruits.
My voice you shall hear in the morning, oh Lord.
In the morning, I will direct it to you. (Psalm 5:3)
David made a vow to make every day a love gift to Me. (Psalm 61:8) All the love you need is found in Me! (Psalm 62:12)

Declare.
Plant the flag, take the ground, and take the territory for My glory.
Look to Me and let Me touch every area of your life with My love, healing, and power.
Forgive, release, and be free of oppression and strongholds.
Great freedom will come when you open and release.
You will be free to give and receive all I have for you, beloved.

Do not worry or fear that to which I have called you.
I will give you the grace to accomplish it.
You cannot fail, for the I Am is with you.
There is no need to discover anything about yourself.
I have given you everything you need...
seek Me, and I will uncover everything I have already deposited in you, My child.

Day 18

My Child...

Consider the cost, My child.
For who would construct a house before first sitting down to estimate the cost to complete it? Paul learned and understood that everything is worthless compared to the infinite value of knowing My Son, Jesus Christ, as Lord.

The value of gaining Jesus is above all.
There is a cost.
Surrender all to Me, give up everything.
Be willing to die to self,
and be filled to overflowing with living water.
You have the choice...to what degree are you willing to go?

There's always more.
There's always another level.
Walk with Me on this journey.
Surrender all. Trust Me.
Consider...and be willing to be joyful together.

Day 19

My Child...

I am the refining fire.
Allow Me to refine you and remove all the dross from your life...
impurity that is not from Me and hinders you.
What the enemy has stolen, he must pay recompense.
Open your mouth and demand payment.
Demand recompense. (Luke 14:23-24)

Day 20

My Child...

My Beloved, your life is not your own.
There are eyes on you. Those in the world are watching you.
Your heart must align with Mine to be the example...
to be the salt and the light to the world.
Their eyes are on you,
your eyes are on Me, and My eyes are on you.

Open your mouth wide and begin to direct your life.
You follow Me because I am your good Shepherd.
Your life is directed by My Word and your declaration. Make sure they align, or your direction will be off from your shepherd.
I will guide you along the best pathway for your life.
I will advise you and watch over you.

I am the God who sees.
I see you, and I know you.
Know this, beloved, I am so pleased with you.

Day 21

My Child...

I will pour water on him who is thirsty.
I will pour floods in the areas of your life that are dry ground.
Keep your eyes on things above and not on earthly things.
You shall find the supernatural in Me.

Pray to Me, *"Father, I am thirsty and want to be filled.*
You are the supernatural miracle-working God.
I want to see your breakthrough in My life."

Day 22

My Child...

Yes, and amen.
Again, I say, "*Yes, and amen*." (2 Corinthians 1:20)
All My promises to you are "yes, and amen."

Beloved, you will feel full and complete when you surrender to Me and allow the Holy Spirit to minister to others by the gifts flowing out of and at work in you. You will feel the joy of knowing and understanding you were created for this.

I have given you the ability to enjoy walking out your purpose.
It will bring such fullness and wholeness.
Just ask.

Day 23

My Child...

Holiness and purity are precious in My sight.
It is what I desire for you. Since you have these promises,
purify yourself from everything that contaminates body and spirit,
perfecting holiness out of reverence for Me. (2 Corinthians 7:1)

The enemy is not afraid of your gifts. He is afraid of your holiness.
Search yourself...search your heart and allow the Holy Spirit to
correct you. We correct those we love.
Those who know Me and have made Me Lord of their life
will receive My correction with joy, knowing it will bring more
freedom, growth, and revelation.
I release my blessing proportionate to the character you have
allowed Me to develop in you.
Be holy, for I am holy. (1 Peter 1:16)

Follow Me. Walk like I do.
It is for your benefit and protection.
Put the Word in you so richly that it will go deep and produce
great fruit. You are My fruitful vine...whole and filled, overflowing.

Day 24

My Child...

My beloved, wide is the gate, and broad is the way that
leads to destruction. Many are going through it.
Keep your eyes fixed and steady upon Me.

As you walk with Me, I will continue to take you to deeper levels.
As you yield in every area of your life, the revelation will flow
freely. As you align with and believe My Word over and above
everything else that is coming into your heart and mind that is of
this world, we will walk as one, just as I am three in one...the
Father, Son, and Holy Spirit. You live and move and have
your being in Me.

Small is the gate, and narrow is the way that leads to life.
I desire for you to live an abundant life.
Beloved, settle for nothing less.
When you ask, seek...knock...there will always be a "*Yes, and
Amen.*" When you seek Me, I will be found by you.

Dream about the depths and heights you want to go to with Me.
There are no limits for you and Me.
Get free from any limitations you feel are from this earthly realm.
Address them. Surrender them to Me and confess them to others.
Limitations must not be allowed to have their way in your life.

I am jealous for you, beloved.
I want you all for myself, every inch, every emotion.
I want all the joy, all the pain.
I want all of you...I love and created you.
I don't want any part of you oppressed or unhealed, so press in.
This is your time...this is your time.

...continued.

I sing My songs of freedom over you, and I release My fullness.
Be an amazing receiver and receive all I am and all I have for you.
Respond to Me, beloved.
Do your part. I am always faithful to do Mine.

I bid you to come, step out of your box onto the water with Me.
Fix your eyes on Me, and you will walk freely and lightly with
strength and purity. I love you and bid you to come to Me.

Day 25

My Child...

You were designed to be with Me in fellowship and unity.
You do not belong in this broken world.
You do not fit within this broken system, but it has a purpose.
Every day is a gift that I give and provide.

Make the most of life and be careful how you live.
Do not be like those without understanding.
Live honorably and true with godly wisdom...
or you are living in evil times.
Take full advantage of each day as you spend your life for My purposes. (Ephesians 5:16)

One drop will spoil.
One drop will infiltrate and penetrate.
You have one life.
You get to choose life or death, blessings or curses.
Will you live as a victim or a victor?
A real and present enemy is working against all My children,
but the price has been paid.
The outcome is known and written in My book.

Are you an overcomer or are you being overcome by this world?
Ask these questions, beloved.
Search your heart and judge yourself.
Get the answers to these questions.
You have one life, what will you do with what you have been given? What will you do with what has been deposited within you?
Allow Me to be a light to your path and order your steps.
Give Me everything,
and I will overwhelm you with everything I am for you.
I can multiply and redeem the time.
I make all things new.
Is My arm too short to save, heal, or restore?
I am only limited by you, beloved.
If you struggle with unbelief, I can help with that, too. Just ask.

Day 26

My Child...

I am your all-sufficient one.
Let your heart not be troubled by this world or by your circumstances. I have overcome this world, and as I am, so are you.
That means you are also an overcomer, beloved.
For it is I that works in you, to will and to do, for My good pleasure.

Empty yourself to Me.
Allow Me to be all things for you in all situations.
Allow Me to penetrate the places that are holding you.
Freedom is your inheritance and your birthright.
Jesus has set you free.
Speak and declare it over your life and circumstances.

Day 27

My Child...

As you connect with Me in the spirit...
A path is being cleared before you.
I go before you, removing things that have not yet been removed.
A supernatural exchange is happening as you connect with Me in this posture.

As you rest in Me and allow Me to minister to you in the spirit, chains are loosed...chains are breaking.
A calm will come, and you will have my grace to walk through things that have been a stumbling block for you in the past.
This will allow you to occupy a new space and territory that carries with it new permissions and freedoms.
A calm grace is here for you to walk differently than before.

Have no regrets, beloved.
Just walk before Me, connecting in the spirit, and things will move...things will happen.
You may not feel it or sense it, but the breakthrough is at hand.
The Breaker is breaking through for you.
Thank Me and receive it as you already have it.

Your prayer and worship are a sweet aroma to Me.
I receive them from you.
I am generous in giving and receiving.
As you pray, the darkness is being pushed out, and your territory is expanding. The kingdom of heaven is forcefully advancing, and the strong take it by force. (Matthew 11:12)

In the spirit, you are a fierce warrior.
My fire is coming upon you, burning up all the chaff.
I am purifying you by My fire.
You are being prepared like a bride for Me, without spot or wrinkle.
I am always with you, beloved.
Have no fear and go forth as one who is sent.
You are My sent one.
You are Mine, My dear one.

Day 28

My Child...

Freedom, I sing a song of freedom over you today.
My Son has set you free, and you are free indeed. (John 8:36)
It is for freedom that Jesus Christ has set you free...
so do not let yourself be burdened again by a yoke of slavery.
Arise, I say to you. Shake off the dust and sit in a place of honor.
Break off the shackles of bondage from around your neck.

The life that pleases Me is lived in the gratitude of grace,
always choosing to walk with Me in what is right.
This choice is the sacrifice I desire from you.
Do this, and the benefits of My salvation will unfold to you.

Day 29

My Child...

My Son finished His work.
After He said upon the cross, "It is finished,"
He bowed His head and gave up His spirit. (John 19:30)
In the same way, I am at work in you, giving you the desire
and the power to do what pleases Me. (Philippians 2:13)

In My Kingdom, last is first, burdens are light,
death is life, losing is gaining, and sorrow is Joy.
Mine is a divine exchange, beloved.
Celebrate that you can give Me everything that is broken,
in despair, worrisome, damaged, forgotten, and alone.
I made it new.
I see the value when no one else does.
Nothing is a loss in My Kingdom.
I can breathe life into all things.

Don't miss out.
You have not because you have asked Me for nothing.
I can bring your dreams back that you thought were gone.
Resurrection is available to you.
As He is, so are you in this life.

Day 30

My Child...

The world is broken and wants you to align yourself with it.
It's like swimming upstream to walk with Me in this world.
Even though you feel vulnerable as a lamb going into a pack of wolves, remember, it is I who sends you out.
Be as shrewd as a serpent, yet as harmless as a dove.
Don't worry if you feel lost at times or as if you are going down the wrong road.
For I am with you...I will never leave you nor forsake you.

There is no lack.
I have given you everything you need for this life and godliness. (2 Peter 1:3) I want to give you overflowing joy.
Allow My joy to be your strength.
There are no limitations on you.
A great cloud of witnesses surrounds you...the saints of the past who have gone before you watch as you run your race.
They are cheering you on to victory.
Trials are meant to strengthen you and your faith.
Allow them to bring you to maturity.
Persevere...put your hand to the plow and don't look back.
Run your race, My dear child.

Day 31

My Child...

Come to Me, all that are heavy laden with burdens.
I will refresh your life, for I am your oasis. (Matthew 11:28)
The depths of My love are so great, beloved.

Cast all your cares upon Me.
Trust and give them to Me, for there is a grace for you and a freedom available. It is not yours to carry. It is yours to give Me.
A living sacrifice, pleasing to Me.

Sit in My presence...worship Me.
Give Me the best of you, beloved.
The windows of heaven will be poured out on your life.
What you put your hands will be blessed and prosper.
Your father Abraham held nothing back from Me, even to the point of being willing to give Me his son. Just as your father Abraham did, trust Me with all you are and all you have. He knew I was faithful and could raise his son. Isaac was the promise, so he knew I had to be faithful to My Word.

A new level of trust in My faithfulness needs to happen, beloved.
I want you to stay at rest as you walk through this life.
Nothing can steal your peace as you walk in tandem with Me.
Jesus is your Prince of Peace. He covers you when you come to the end of yourself and your striving.
I want to do all things for you...I can do all things for you.

Hear that, beloved.
Feel the weight of My glory on you.
You were never meant to live your life outside of Me.
You live and move and have your being in Me.
That is where you will feel the best and be your best...only in Me.
Search your heart for what you have not yet surrendered to Me.
Allow Me in to touch every area of your being.

Day 32

My Child...

I anoint your head with fresh anointing oil this morning.
Jesus is the anointed oil poured forth. (Song of Solomon 1:2)
Just as Moses anointed Aaron and consecrated his position as high priest, feel the anointing flowing over you this morning.
You are set apart...holy for My purposes.

You are equipped for every good work, My child.
I equip you for that which I called you.
You will never fall short or be put to shame...
for your hope and trust in Me.

As you are on your journey, sojourning on this earth,
ask, seek, knock. Do not grow cold or stop.
Press on and put your hand to the plow.
Don't look back.
I don't take you backward.

In My Kingdom, we run forward in the race.
You will not grow weary. You will not faint.
The enemy wants you to look back to stop your forward momentum, but I have natural and spiritual laws in place.
A thing in motion stays in motion...a thing at rest stays at rest.
My Kingdom is forward movement through this life.

Picture a pond that collects water and sits dormant versus a river that runs and flows...being useful... providing water, food, and fish.
It is a source of good.

You are that source of good...life speaking, life-giving good.
The river of life flows out of you, beloved.
Free-flowing movement of life.
It is a treasure in you, dear one.

Day 33

My Child...

There is only one God...Me, the Father.
I am the source of all things, and your lives are to be lived for Me.
There is one Lord, Jesus...the anointed One through whom all things exist. You are My expensive and priceless purchase...
paid for with tears of blood.

Your response of love and worship to Me is to use your body, your temple, to bring Me glory.
I will equip you for that which I have called you to.
Be single-minded...focused on Me and My Word.
The things that occupy your time and energy will be taken care of.
The more you give Me, the more I pour out revelation, direction, and divine appointments.

Meditate on My Word.
Wait and listen to the Rhema words I have given you.
Let them get into your spirit man so deep that they will take root and grow into a substance that produces fruit.
Allow the Word to live in you so richly.

Many things fight for your time and attention.
You must become aware of when the enemy is having his way in your life to keep you from this assignment of putting Me first.
Become aware. Blinders must be removed in this area.
Settle it in your heart that you will tithe a portion of your day to Me. I will receive and honor this, beloved.

Give Me your life as a holy sacrifice.
There is no greater peace, joy, and exhilaration than fulfilling the destiny I have written for you in your book.
That is the most fulfilling thing you will do during this time on the earth...doing what you were created for.

...continued.

You are an arrow in My hand.
When you go forth, you will hit your mark.
I know your every need, and you will lack nothing.
You will hit your mark. I will equip you and provide for you.
You will hit your mark. You have what you need in Me.
I am My beloved's, and My beloved is Mine.

Day 34

My Child...

I am the light of the world.
I am in you, and you are in Me.
You are My hands and feet.
You are the light in this world.
Beloved, let your light shine so brightly before others that your commendable works will be as light upon them.
Then they will give their praise to Me in heaven.

Beloved, how can people call on Me for help if they do not believe?
How can they believe if they have not heard?
How can they hear My Message of life if no one proclaims it?
I am pouring out My grace upon you to proclaim and share.

People's hardness will be softened by the words of grace that come from your mouth. Your life will be a light to them...a place of comfort and encouragement. People who give their ear to you will hear you speak grace-filled words.
They will drip with My peace and glory.
They will be heard, and their words pondered.
They will produce fruit of light that will remove blinders and bring the backslidden and the wounded back to the fold.
My desire...My heart is for them.

So, I give you the grace today.
I touch your tongue with My finger to anoint.
You are Mine...I redeemed you. I give you My grace today.

Day 35

My Child...

I anoint you and grant you wisdom for the fight.
You are in this earthly realm...
so don't be surprised when you are wounded.
I promised you the victory...
I never promised you wouldn't get wounded in the battle. (John 16:33) I told you in this world you will have tribulations, trials, and sorrows. You must allow yourself to be seated with Me in the heavenly realm. Rise above all the worries, cares, and pulls of this world. Rest in Me, for I fight for you, beloved.
Not in your power but in My limitless love and power.

I renew you...you will have enough.
You will conquer, no matter the circumstances.
You were created in My image.
You are the righteous.
I hear you and deliver you from your troubles. (Psalm 34:17)
My eyes are on you.
Be faithful...be obedient to Me in all things,
and I will lift you up and advance you.

Do not fight Me or be angry at Me for your circumstances.
Be still and see the salvation of the Lord.
Fight to stay innocent and soft as a child.
Every hard place be softened in My love.
I purchased you at a high price.
Your value and worth are so precious to Me.
I want your life to be so full and joyful that you overflow...
I bought that overflow for you.
That price has been paid. Don't live below that, beloved.

You are the example for others as you live in Me.
Follow Me so they will follow the Jesus in you.
We must live so differently, victoriously.
Surrender every area that keeps you from that place.
Put it under the blood and allow it to be dealt with.
Nothing hidden...nothing left in darkness.

Day 36

My Child...

I will never leave you nor forsake you.
I walk with you down every road and through every trial.
I am with you in every pit and valley, and on your most joyful days.
I share it all with you, My love.
Your frustrations and anxiousness are easy for Me.
They are a joy because you reach for Me in trials...
then I can be all things for you in all situations.

Don't try to understand everything, for there are mysteries.
I am a spirit, and you are a spirit being as well.
The natural cannot explain the spirit, beloved.
Relax and let go of all your expectations and striving.
Don't allow yourself to think, *"I should be here by now."*
What can't I do for you in a moment?
I am the creator of all things and of you.
I own the cattle on a thousand hills. (Psalm 50:10)
Every blessing is yours.
I hold nothing back when you are ready to receive.

Allow Me to be your source for everything and in all situations.
Not an afterthought, but your first thought, your first instinct to bring Me in, to seek My face, counsel, protection, and comfort.
I have all you need.
I am everything for you and in all things.
One drop in your cup, and your cup will be running over.
You decide how much of Me you get.
Don't let that be stolen from you.

Day 37

(From the author: I had a vision of a covering being removed that had been placed upon us by the enemy.)

My Child...

I am jealous for you.
Not a worldly jealousy, but a godly jealousy. (2 Corinthians 11:2)
I want nothing between us...no obstacles or hindrances.
I will go before you and be the breaker that breaks through.
I freed you, so stand fast and do not be entangled again with the yoke of bondage. You worry about too many things.
Too many things occupy your heart and thoughts.

He who My Son has set free is free indeed.
You are sons and daughters grafted into My family.
I know everything about you. I created you just as you are.
I enjoy you and want pure and intimate fellowship with you.
Hold nothing back from Me.

Your inheritance is great and rich.
You cannot serve two masters.
Choose in your heart to give all to Me.
You can't have fear...that is not of Me.
My inheritance is rich for you.
Don't choose the world over Me. Put away all the fruit of the flesh.
It's a process of renewal that I want to walk through with you.
Draw all you need from My deep, unending source.
I am here for you.

Day 38

My Child...

Zeal for your house consumes Me.
You must lose yourself to gain everything.
Eat My Word, and it will become your joy and your heart's delight. (Jeremiah 15:16) I always satisfy the soul of the thirsty one, and I fill the hungry with goodness. (Psalm 107:9)

All the dullness must be washed away, beloved.
You must be a flame of fire, burning with My holy fire.
You are under My new covenant.
I give you all My goodness and the fullness of My Kingdom.
My covenant breaks the yoke of the enemy.
I put My law in you and wrote it on your heart.

My Spirit gives life.
Set your mind on things of the Spirit, and you will live and walk in the fullness of My Spirit...you will not stumble.
You are not under the law...you are under My grace.
You are a new creation in Me, and the old things have passed away. Remember them no more...
I paid the price and washed them away.

Day 39

My Child...

My thoughts are not your thoughts, and your ways are not
My ways. You can't fathom how I do things.
The Israelites saw no way forward and thought it was their end
until I parted the sea. Your thoughts are natural thoughts.
Come up and see life from My heavenly perspective.
You don't know a way or a solution...
but your Father who loves you is not limited by anything.
I am never at a loss or a dead end.

I am pleased by your faith.
I marvel at great faith.
That which is not of faith is sin. (Romans 14:23)
Put away the things of this world...separate yourself.
Do not fear the quietness or loneliness.
Do not think that you are missing out.
You are set apart, holy, for My purposes...by My desire and design.

The time is short...you are needed.
Faith has been deposited in you. Faith comes by hearing.
Take Me in, breathe Me in, and join yourself to Me.
Meditate on My Word and study My character...My ways.
I am your all in all.

Day 40

My Child...

I have placed My gifts and understanding in you.
You are effective in My Kingdom.
What you have is needed. Never belittle or make yourself small.

My Word is meant to frame your world to ensure you stay within the proper boundaries. My Word should frame your words and your mind. Be aware and recognize when you are speaking and thinking in opposition. Do not allow this in your life. When we are in agreement in these areas, you will run your race with speed, grace, and endurance because it is how you were designed to operate. Otherwise, it's like doing 50 mph in third gear.

I formed and fashioned you, dear one.
You are My great creation.
You are being continually interceded for. You have your very own cheering section and advocates in heaven, wanting you to break through and get the victory.
Finish your race strong...hide this truth in your heart so it refreshes you when you are tired and weary.

Allow My discipline and correction in your life. Do not fight it.
Receive it...for I discipline those I love.
I know you want to change and to grow.
I know your joy when I use you to touch a life.
Be patient and gentle in correction.
It's the door you must go through for change to come.
It is always easier to partner with Me in this.

You are being perfected and made into My image.
Don't mistake that for anything else.
The devil wants to use this growth process against you to make you feel "less than." He did it to Jesus in the desert, saying, *"If you are the Son of God..."* when he knew fully who Jesus was.
You must fight to protect and walk in your identity, My child.

Day 41

(From the author: I had a vision of tongues of fire as the Bible describes tongues resting on each person. Then I saw the tongues on fire, but it was on our hearts.)

My Child...

I am a consuming fire.
When you have a problem or an issue in your life, you must overcome and get the victory. It looks daunting and big to you... but to Me, it is a small thing...a simple house of cards.
When you sit in My presence, learn to rest in Me and soak in Me, and that impossible thing will fade away.
Don't try to understand...trust in Me.
One plus one is two in the natural...
but I multiply and extend in My realm.
I make the old things new...the imperfect things perfect.

I see a way where there doesn't seem to be a way.
I make roads in the desert.
Do not fear or be troubled by anything.
I have you in the palm of My hand.
I have written your purpose and plans in your book.
I am your creator, maker, and lover of your soul.
I am for you.

I have prepared a way of escape from temptations and troubles.
Refuse to worry or be anxious.
It is the enemy warring against you when it rears its head.
Make no room for it in your heart or life.
I am pleased when you choose to trust and have faith
that I will meet your needs.
Just like the father ran to his prodigal son when he chose wisely,
I will run to meet your need...to pour out to overflowing.
It is My joy to give you My all.
It is My pleasure to see you overflow.
Stir up the gifts I have given you.
That holy fire is yours.
You need the fire from the altar today.

Day 42

My Child...

I always remain faithful, for I cannot deny who I am.
I am faithful. (2 Timothy 2:13)
Study My Word and put it deep in your heart.
Be one who correctly explains My Word of truth.
When you trust in Me, I will keep you in perfect peace.
Do your part, for I am always faithful to do My part.

Areas where you carry worry or anxiety are not surrendered
to Me yet. My peace must rule in your heart.
I gave you your personality and emotions to enjoy life and laugh.
You were never designed to be ruled by your emotions.
Your spirit must be the one you allow to rule.
Trust Me with all your heart,
don't lean on your own understanding.
I search your heart and examine the secret motives.
I reward you according to your actions.

You were called out of darkness to the light to be a blessing and
obtain blessings. (1 Peter 2:9; 3:9)
Do not fear, for I can make the crooked paths straight.
I make all things new.
I know the end from the beginning.
I am good and have given you a good end...I am good to you.

Day 43

My Child...

Your value to Me is priceless.
You have been given some ability and strength to accomplish things in your own power, but it is limited and falls far below your destiny. Walk in tandem with Me and with fellow believers that can sharpen you. This life is not meant to be lived outside your brothers and sisters of the faith. I place key people in your life. Receive them and walk with them.
Don't give just anyone a high place in your life...
give only to those who love Me and are seeking Me with all their heart, soul, mind, and strength.

Two are better than one because there is a good reward and return for their labor. And if you fall, the one will lift the other. One can chase a thousand, and two can put ten thousand to flight. There is a harvest, so put your hand to the plow and don't look back. Drive forward. Take the territory one step at a time.
I am with you, and we can take much ground.

Day 44

My Child...

All I have I give to you. I hold nothing back.
You are Mine, and it pleases Me to bless My own.
It is the anointing that breaks the yoke of bondage.
You have been yoked by the enemy in some way. It's why the struggles are always there...lurking in the shadows and sometimes in full light. It is all the enemy's yoke...whether it's the lie, "You're not good enough..." or "You're no good..." or just a constant lack or feeling like everyone else is moving, growing, and accomplishing except you. Don't believe any of those lies.

You are Mine. I thought of you, and I created you in My image.
You lack nothing.
The work I began in you will be brought to completion.
You are loved perfectly and completely.
You are adored and thought of continuously.

More than the grains of sand on the seashore...laugh at the struggle and look to Me. We can overcome it together.
I have already overcome this world, so everything is subject to you, including your feelings.
It may not seem like it, but feelings do not rule you.
You are a spirit being ruled by the Spirit.
Be gentle on yourself and be your own fan.
You have a cheering section in your homeland of heaven and an advocate Who is always praying for you.
How you see yourself matters in this life, My child.

See yourself how I see you.
Come up to My higher thoughts so the process can be enjoyed.
I did not design life to be enjoyed only when you reach a milestone, such as having a certain position or amount of money.
Enjoy every moment of this walk...
You only have one life and then all eternity with Me.

...continued.

Make the most of your days. Hug your loved ones and step out when I prompt you.
Don't shrink back.

You are a child of the Lion of the Tribe of Judah, and My righteous ones are as bold as Lions. When your mindset aligns with Me and My Word...it's like having a key that unlocks all the doors so you can walk easily through.

Day 45

My Child...

As the lifting of another veil, another level...
I crowned you with My goodness.
Your inheritance as My sons and daughters is so great.
You are thought about and provided for.
You have a high priest Who is Jesus who knows every wound and hurt. He experienced it all...He understands and relates.
As He is, so are you.

Goodness and mercy follow you every day of your life.
Look for it, expect it...it is part of your inheritance.
Don't spend a moment of your time and energy in regret or guilt.
I give every day as a gift, and My mercies are new every day.
I don't cover sin...I take it away as though it never happened.
All things can be restored and made into something new.

I am jealous for you with a godly jealousy.
I don't want to share your heart space with guilt, pain, or regret.
I want a heart full of devotion that is quick to return to Me and repent. Can you see through My heavenly lens and adjust your mindset to understand that it takes away from Me when you are bogged down?

He who the son sets free is free indeed.
So, refuse to go back into the bondage of your past.
When you are free, your reach is far and wide.
Your prayers go into different realms and generations.
Grasp the importance. You are needed.
I have placed you here for such a time as this.

Day 46

My Child...

Your eyes have not seen, your ears have not heard, and your mind has not imagined the many things I have in store for you.
I delight in you, and I will establish your every step.
You will be secure and sure-footed when your trust is in Me...always...in every situation...like the legs of a deer that can run and jump effortlessly as though light as air.

Walk by faith, not by your natural sight or instinct.
It is time to go deeper with Me.
You are ready to receive more.
You were not designed for measure, beloved.
You are not limited.

Day 47

My Child...

Simplify.
Many things hold your attention and focus. Many things busy you. Observe and take stock of it all. Reprioritize with a Kingdom mindset and perspective. Just as Jesus pointed out to Martha, you are worried and upset, pulled away by many distractions. There is only one thing that is important and worth being concerned about.

Do not fall into the trap of love for this world
and the things it offers.
Your worth, value, and love all come from Me.
I set your feet upon the rock and make your steps secure.
My love is not based on your performance.
My love is not qualified or pulled away.
My love is constant, perfect, and all-consuming.
Bask in My love...meditate on it and receive it.

Day 48

My Child...

People often think they are doing the right things in their own eyes, but I examine the heart and the motives.
Be sober-minded and watchful.
Have pillars in your life. They help you weigh decisions and act wisely, and they help you protect and consider people.
Let the fruit of the spirit be evident in your life.
You should be known by your fruit.
Practice the art of encouragement and drawing out the good in others...learning to call them up.

My words are creative.
I have given you the ability as My child to speak into existence, to call things forth.
A word rightly spoken is like apples of gold in settings of silver.
Become a master builder of people's lives with your words.
Point the way to Me.

Pass through...go from old to new.
Prepare a new path for people.
Build up a highway for them to come to Me.
Remove every hindrance...remove the stones.
Pull out the boulders and lift a standard over the people.

Day 49

My Child...

Just as Jesus had nowhere to lay his head,
you will never feel 100% at home in this world.
Don't be discouraged by this, for just as Jesus came to have his appointed time on this earth to fulfill His purpose and plan...
so must you.

There is so much joy and wonder to be had during this lifetime.
Have eyes to see it all as joy.
Observe and watch a leaf fall onto a gently moving stream.
It is carried on top of the water, moving with the flow around bends and rocks, letting itself be taken on the stream's journey.
In the same way, rest in Me...
allow Me to carry you through your life's journey.
I have your answers. I have the roadmap.
I am a generational God, showing unfailing lovingkindness for a thousand generations to those who love and obey Me.

Day 50

My Child...

I gave an answer to your time in this life through the parable of the servants and talents. I gave them talents just as I have given you talents in the form of spiritual gifts and the Holy Spirit.
What will you do with My Spirit who dwells so richly in you?
What will you do with My Son?
I have designed you to impact others.
You were pulled from darkness to light to be a blessing.
Bless others with your kindness, valuing them as one of Mine...
as one that I created and breathed My breath of life into.

Look hard into people...look beyond the flesh and see their inner heart, not their outward man that may look polished and made-up. Look beyond and minister to what you see, or the lack you see, for I have made you kings and priests.
It is through you that I work, beloved.
Through you, I love the hurting and the lost.
Living water pours through you to bring the dead things back to life. Understand that sometimes, the smallest act of faithfulness restores hope in others. It matters how you live, love, and speak. It matters to Me...and those you don't realize are closely watching.

Allow Me to touch your heart and heal every wound.
Speak to Me in your hurt that I may bring restoration.
I am your source. Let Me love you.
With Me, you are safe and can be real...your truest self.
With the personality I created and gave you.

Day 51

My Child...

The veil was torn, and the way was made for you.
I lifted the burden from you.
My burden is easy and light.
I have made the crooked places straight in your life.
Those who are the sons of the devil are full of deceit and fraud...
they continue to make crooked the straight ways I have made.
(Acts 13:10)

Do you live in the world, where two kingdoms exist and clash?
It is easy to fall into confusion because of the work being
done by each kingdom simultaneously.
Fix your gaze upon Me.
Steady your emotions and join your spirit with Mine daily.
Walk closely with Me, and there will be no space for the enemy to
occupy in your life.

All things are revealed to Me.
All things are bare and exposed by Me. (Hebrews 4:13)
I know the difficulties and pull of this world.
My eyes are upon you.
I have marked you...you are My special treasure.

Day 52

My Child...

Single-mindedness is your key...
focus on Me and My Kingdom.
Eliminate...simplify your life.
There must be a fierce pursuit of intimacy with Me,
and time spent in My Word.
There is a constant pull by the enemy to keep you from Me and our intimacy. Fight to stay in Me...it is part of your journey to maturity.
Connect with My Spirit. Keep Me in front of you...
seeing Me, speaking My Word, and walking with Me.
Let heaven and My Kingdom invade your life.
There are things I want to do for you when this happens.

Day 53

My Child...

My words are life to you.
My Word is health to your body and strength to your bones.
I have formed and fashioned you. You are who I have declared
you to be, not who the world says you are.
There is no shifting or turning in Me.
I am the same yesterday, today, and forever.
The same is true for you.
No matter what situation you find yourself in,
you are Mine, made in My image.
There is goodness, love, peace, joy, and fullness in you.

You have a great capacity for love.
Love that has the power to change the course of people's lives,
for love covers a multitude of sins. Love bears all things, believes
all things, hopes all things, endures all things. The love that comes
through you is the greatest, most powerful thing. Choose to bless
others as I have blessed you.

When you respond and choose to love, I receive it as praise.
I receive it as your love for Me.
Crucify your flesh...lay your life down, My child.
Watch what I will do for you in this life and eternity.
For what you do now is determining your eternity.
Receive this as joy, not as pressure, beloved.
There is a depth beyond what you know...
a reservoir so deep the fruit of the spirit flows like a waterfall.

Day 54

My Child...

Mary discovered the most important thing by
choosing to sit at My feet, and it was not taken from her.
I am your birthright...dive deep into Me.
Swim in My Word...soak in My presence.
I am a deep reservoir for you.
I am a never-ending resource for your life. I stand and wait for you to come near and seek My face.
I always hear and act for you, beloved.

The world and the people of the world will bring opportunities to worry your heart, stress your body, and trouble your soul.
Are you surprised when a bird flies or a fish swims?
That is the character and nature of the world...It is troubling,
so don't be surprised by it.
You are in the world, but not of the world.
You are something new, never before seen on this earth.
I am in you, and you are in Me.
Goodness and Mercy will follow you all the days of your life.
Your path is lit.
Simply walk with Me.
All is well.

Day 55

My Child...

Assurance...assurance in Me. (Psalm 121:3)
You are guarded and guided.
I will never let you stumble or fall.
I am your keeper...I watch over you.
I will never forget you or ignore you.
Upon the rock of Jesus Christ, the church is built.
You are the church, beloved, and the gates of hell shall not prevail against you...shall not overpower you.
You are the victor because Jesus is the Victor.

The power is in the cross.
Boast in the cross.
Be proclaimers of the excellency of Him who called you.
You are chosen and provided for, so do not speak lack when provision is all around.
Abundance is your inheritance.
Speak the language of heaven...
peace, joy, and righteousness.
Come in power and authority.
You are in Me, and I am in you. Carry that assurance with you always and allow it to be bigger than the shortcomings you feel, or the words spoken by the devil. Walk in that assurance.

Day 56

My Child...

Be soaked and drenched with living waters flowing out of your belly. Rivers of living water can bring the dead things back to life and bring the backslidden close again.
Open your mouth wide and I will fill it.
Ask and I will give generously, for I am your portion.
Speak and it will happen when it's according to My will.
I gave you My peace...peace in your mind...
peace in your heart...so do not be troubled or afraid.
If your mind is spinning, declare the peace I gave you over it.
Declare with great authority. It is your birthright.

Day 57

My Child...

Your job is to believe.
Believe that I exist...that I reward those who diligently seek Me.
Believe what you ask in prayer...believe that you have received it, and it will be yours. Whoever believes in Me shall never thirst.
All things are possible to him who believes.
You walk by faith, not by sight.
If you believe, you will see My glory.
Believe Me for the dreams you are dreaming.
I have written and planned for your life and future.
My desire and heart for you is greater than you can ask or imagine.

You are seated with Me in heavenly places...living your life for My Kingdom on this earth. The darkness is increasing, so I lift up a standard for you, giving more grace and glory over your life.
Access it by believing.

Day 58

My Child...

Unity. One joined to another in the spirit realm...
one mind, one heart for My Kingdom.
Declare My Word to Me.
My Word will accomplish what I have purposed.
The breakthrough and victory are yours.
Keep moving forward, step-by-step, methodically...
at times by inches...at times by leaps and bounds,
but always moving and never stagnant.

My kingdom doesn't look back.
The enemy wants you to look back at past mistakes,
regrets, and hurts. My kingdom doesn't look back.
It looks forward...moving ahead...taking ground.
I see you...every tear and every act of kindness.
I am with you. I comfort you and celebrate with you.
I see your sacrifices and hear your prayers.
I bless you in all you do. I prosper your ways.

Day 59

My Child...

Your love is a gift to Me.
I rejoice when you hear My voice and Word...when you are obedient to Me. When you spend time seeking Me and when you hunger for Me, I receive it as devotion and love.
It is part of My reward, for I paid a great price for you, and it is My due that I receive wholeheartedly.
I have only good for My children.

I want to teach you, lead you, comfort you...be all for you.
I have left no stone unturned where you are concerned.
I have you in the palm of My hand.
You are the apple of My eye.
Your place is in Me.
You are secure, loved, and valued.

Trust these things even when you don't feel it.
I have made provision for you. It's all around.
There are no hoops to jump through, nothing to perform.
Just believe it and believe Me.
Let My peace still your heart and watch over your mind. When you remain in Me, the things of this world don't have pull or strength.

Day 60

My Child...

Before you call, I will answer.
While you are still speaking, I will hear.
My ear is inclined to you.
My Kingdom is at hand.
A deep well, an oasis in a dry and thirsty land.
I am not silent or far off from you.
I am as close as your next breath.
Incline your ear to Me...
come in close to hear My thoughts and plans for you.

Call to Me and I will show you great and mighty things, which you do not know. Learn to live in the posture of seeking Me.
Let nothing derail you.
It is now. I am looking for those who are available to Me.
Rejoice in Me. That is exactly what you were created for...
to know Me and to be known by Me.
You are the perfect fit, size, stature, and personality.
You are exactly what I want.

Day 61

My Child...

There is no struggle in My Kingdom...glory to glory...grace to Grace. Remember the Shunamite woman who could have responded in the natural when asked about her son who had died, yet she responded in the spiritual, by faith, that "All is well." In this world, you too will have tribulations that are trials and sorrows, but I have overcome this world. Believe from that place. Pray from that place.

This mindset change will give you effective and powerful prayers and victory. As My child, you are meant to overcome. It is not My plan or My best for you when the contrary happens.
Be up above.
When you are obedient to Me and enter hardship, I am there.
Press into Me...you will not be overtaken...you are a victor.
My promises are *"Yes, and Amen."*

All is well.
You will come through as pure gold, refined as My fire.
Your words and prayers must come from that fire burning up all the chaff from peoples' lives, setting them in freedom.

Day 62

My Child...

Be faithful to Me. Your faith pleases Me.
Your faith speaks in a loud voice to others.
You live a seemingly quiet life,
but it goes forth as a mighty surge to people's hearts and lives.
Believe My Word and have faith in it. It is your very life.
Trust it more than you trust in your next breath or thought.

The floodgates are open to those who are able.
There is simple beauty all around you.
Find the joy in Me, beloved.
I have placed joy all around for you.
As you read about the faith warriors in My Word,
I read about your life as a faith warrior. Stand, beloved, stand.

Day 63

My Child...

I have equipped you to do the work of the ministry.
Let My Spirit strengthen you and work through you.
Connect with Me, your life-giving branch, so I can nurture you...
care directly for you...impart to you. I am your source.

There is nothing I ask you to do in your own power or apart from
Me. So do not fear. Hunt fear down and cast it out of your life.
It is your right as My child to live free.
I have set you free from the flesh and the pulls of this world.
Make war and set yourself against any other voice speaking
to you except Mine.

I will only speak life. Even when I bring correction or conviction,
it is in love and to build you up.
There is no condemnation when I speak.
I am life-giving...I am abundance...I am living water to you.
Keep believing in Me and ask without ceasing until you feel peace
and receive what you are asking for. The enemy wants you to grow
discouraged and your heart to grow sick. Beloved, it's a trap!
For My ear is inclined to you...I hear you.
I know you care so deeply.

I know the end from the beginning,
so, you must trust Me in each situation.
Do not ask Me why...just walk and trust.
Stay connected, and I will work all things for your good.
You will come through a fire purified as pure gold.

Day 64

(From the author: I had a vision of a full table.)

My Child...

Compel them to come.
How can they hear unless they are told?
How can they be told unless you love them enough to open your mouth? So, open your mouth wide and I will fill it. I will show you what to speak. Your words will be sweet, dripping with honey, and pleasing to the hearer.

Allow your spirit to be in control. The flesh must decrease...
it must be crucified by your doing. It is your choice alone.
Your spirit man is the true you. You are a spirit being.
You are seated with Me in heavenly places.
The struggle comes when the flesh rises and demands to have its way, but you are an overcomer.
Ask Me for the divine appointments I have for you.
You are a joy, a blessing, a child of the Most High
with a destiny that carries the blessing of heaven.

Day 65

My Child...

I know your heart's desire...that which you are longing for.
I hear you when you think to yourself,
"What's wrong with Me?...Why is this happening?"
Don't be downcast or question your situation.

Give it to Me, for you were not meant to be weighed down
by the cares of this world.
Look to Me and I will work out every situation.
Look to Me and allow My Word to renew your mind and
expectations because the world shapes you and gives you thoughts
that need to be weeded out. They are not of Me or from Me and
they are giving you wrong hopes and expectations.

Do not fear, for I restore and renew.
I make all things new.
My Kingdom must come in your life.
I desire true worshipers who worship Me in spirit and in truth.
I am My beloved's, and My beloved is Mine.

Day 66

My Child...

Why are you downcast? Oh, My soul?
Why do you sink into despair? (Psalm 42:5)
Keep hoping and waiting on Me, your God...your Savior.
Even if everyone leaves you, forsakes you, and disappoints you...
I am always with you.
I have an everlasting love for you.
I think of you and dream of you.
I have planned a destiny and purpose for you.

You are meant for love, joy, and peace.
Do not fear or fret if things do not look as you think they should.
For I am able and willing to do all things...to exceed...to expand.
So, be about My Kingdom, beloved.
I will free you from every entanglement.
I break the bands from around your neck.
Arise and shake off the dust. I am calling you up.
Don't look around at what others are doing. Follow Me.
I desire to lead you in the way you should go.

Day 67

My Child...

My love for you is complete, faithful, and long-suffering.
I overlook the outer to see the true you...your inner man.
Nothing can keep Me from loving you, from pursuing you.
What I have said will be fulfilled.
What can stand in My way?
Nothing can keep Me from blessing you.
I called you out of darkness into the marvelous light
to be a blessing.

When you are ready to hear, I send the answer.
You are not waiting on Me, I am waiting on you.
I am patient and long-suffering.
We can stroll together or run together.
The pace is your choice, just know I am here.

Day 68

My Child...

I must have My will.
You must choose to place yourself under My authority,
surrendering and submitting as a daily act of worship.
Dive in...make those things that seem far off or impossible a reality.
You can't see how it will work or the way that is made,
but I am your way maker...the one who makes springs in the desert.
I am the potter who can recreate and make things new.

From time to time, you catch a glimpse of the plan for your life,
but the cares of this world push it out.
Speak it, believe it, grab hold of it...
allow Me to make it happen as you partner with Me.
I release you unto it. You are free and uninhibited.
Clarity and assurance are given freely.
Ask for a revelation of My goodness.
Ask for the Nations.
Ask beloved, for I am a Father who loves to give and bless you.
I love to bless through holy fire...
holy fire burning up all the chaff in your life...
burning up the confusion.

Have clarity and peace in your mind.
My provision is all around you in abundance...
overflowing, pressed together, and available.
What you ask Me for I say, *"Yes, and Amen."*

Day 69

My Child...

Your faithfulness delights Me.
No more are you tossed to and fro like the waves of the sea.
When I drew you, you responded and received Me.
I planted your feet firmly on the rock.
You are rooted and grounded in Me.
No one and nothing can snatch you from My hand.
At times, you may feel like you are on shifting sand.
Speak to your situation.
Speak to your emotions and align with My Word.
The Kingdom is there.

As you walk with Me through life's situations, you are maturing and being perfected. The things that made you stumble as a new believer do not bother you anymore. This is that.
As you become more Kingdom-minded, and as your flesh decreases, I will increase in your life. Your understanding and revelation will also increase in great measure.

I desire to reveal all to you.
The process of coming out from this world can be a lonely one.
I am with you, and you are greatly loved.
I will bring you all you need and desire.
Be willing to walk through these times with joy and patience knowing it is producing great fruit.

Day 70

My Child...

I am the lifter of your head. I thought of you and breathed you out.
When it is in your power to do good, do not hold back.
You are called to be a blessing.
Do what My Son did...He did good to all.
He was about My business, which is My children and My Kingdom.

I have granted you freedom in My Spirit.
I will come alongside and be with you when you are prompted by your faith to fulfill it all.
Do not look to others or worry what they are doing.
Stand strong and keep your eyes focused on Me and My Word, and your path will be straight. You will have clarity and you will hear My voice directing you in your spirit. Have confidence in that.

Your voice is sweet to My ears. I hear your intercessions. I incline My ear to you, My child. Your faith pleases Me, so do not be discouraged in doing good, for in due time you will reap a reward if you do not lose heart.

Day 71

My Child...

You are under My covering.
You are in My thoughts, and they are too great to number.
Come up to My higher thoughts.
Speak to Me and then speak to your mountains.
Speak where you are going, do not speak your natural circumstances or your current situation.
Come up to My higher thoughts where there are no impossibilities.

It is the timing of things that tend to throw you off.
My timing is perfect and has a purpose.
My desire is to lavish you with everything.
I can only give you what you are prepared for so make your life a living sacrifice, an altar of earth to Me. Give it all to Me.
Do not look to the natural situation to determine what I am doing and what I am not doing...for My ways are higher.
When you have disappointments, you must allow Me to have My way and work all things out for your good.

Commit your ways to Me, for you have escaped the corruption of this world and you are partakers of the divine nature.
By My Spirit, I grant you the favor of Men to draw them into My Kingdom and into our family. I sweeten your words, so the hearers are edified, uplifted, and drawn to Me.

Day 72

My Child...

Do not allow what's happening in the natural affect you spiritually.
Guard your heart. Believe I am able.
Believe I am willing...willing to move and act.
I am your source. I will fill you to overflowing.
The tiredness and discouragement get washed away.
Something great is here...joy is available as a way of life.
Joy is bubbling up within you.

Direct your heart with your spirit.
Trust that you will have all your desires fulfilled.
I am able, and I am willing.
Open your mouth wide to Me and I will fill it.
I am your source. There is no lack in My Kingdom.
You have not because you ask not.
Ask and see how I open the windows of heaven for you.
Stand faithful and joyful during this process.
Let the words of your mouth be sweet and pleasing to My ears.
Let no idle, worthless words come out of your mouth.
Direct your mouth by your spirit.

Day 73

My Child...

Come to Me all who are burdened and heavy laden,
and I will give you rest. You can find rest in Me for your weariness.
It may seem like the wicked prosper and have their way with no consequences, but I see the wicked, and I see My children.
Trust Me to deal with each of them.
Do not allow them to trouble you or take your focus from Me.

Forgive quickly and be free from every hook and snare that would keep you from your purpose and intimacy with Me.
When you encounter Me, I bring peace to situations.
I bring assurance, even if it is correction or something hard to hear.
I give a loving word and a way out.
I am with you through it.
When you have an encounter that is not from Me, you will walk through it with My lamp upon your head as I light your way and walk you through.

Seek godly counsel.
Iron sharpens iron.
I have given you divine relationships.
Some you know and some you don't know yet.
Keep your heart open and be childlike in My Kingdom.

Day 74

My Child...

Swim. Submerge yourself in the knowledge of Me and My Word.
Learn to wait on Me.
Learn to sit still in My presence and hear My voice.
I am your breaker that will break through on your behalf.
I will multiply the least of you into a thousand and the weakest one into a mighty nation. (Isaiah 60:22)
Don't think, "I am nothing special."
You are designed to touch a nation with your prayers and send shockwaves through the spirit realm.

With Me as your strength, you can crush an enemy horde, advancing through every stronghold that stands in front of you. (Psalm 18:29)
See as My eyes see.
Speak as My mouth speaks.
Have ears to hear and be willing to receive correction.
It will help you advance at a quicker pace.
If something of this world is in you or in your midst, don't live with it. You are Mine and I am jealous for you.
Rebuke it, resist it, turn from it.
Keep walking with Me closely and intimately.
If you don't know how, just ask Me, and wait for Me to give you the knowledge, understanding, and revelation.
Ask, for I am willing and able.

Day 75

(From the author: I had a vision of the old-fashioned scales of justice, which showed Me that even when we give a small portion, so much more is poured out...more than we could ask or imagine.)

My Child...

You are seated with Me in the heavenlies.
I want you to take on a heavenly perspective.
The daily issues of life will be seen from a heavenly perspective and mindset, and your spirit man will arise and lead your life.

Love must be your motivator.
You must not allow yourself to be driven by fear, worry, or anxiety.
Sit still and know that I am your God.
Connect with Me and My great love for you...move from that place.
In Me you live, move, and have your being.
From that place, living water flows battles are won.
Release your mind to Me.
Release your expectations to Me.
I have your destiny.
I have your life and they are well cared for.

The measure you give to Me will be given to you, and what you have to give to Me is yourself, your trust, and your time. It is measured by a heavenly scale.

Day 76

My Child...

Spirit of multiplication.
Put away all the unclean things.
Protect your eyes and your ears from the world.
Set yourself apart for Me.
Allow My Spirit to set you on fire.

Day 77

My Child...

Come daily and give Me the cares and burdens of this world.
For what I have spoken about you will happen.
Believe Me for your destiny, for your assignments and purposes.
Focus on being a worshiper of Me.
If you have lack, don't look to people and expect them to be able to fill that void. It is putting a great burden and strain on them.
I have given you everything you will ever need for this life.
Hear that, beloved...everything.

Meditate on My Word.
I will give you understanding and revelation.
I will make your words sweet to people's ears and your tongue gentle. A gentle, pure tongue pleases Me.
You may not feel effective, but as you sit at My feet, your words will begin to have more impact on people's lives.
Speak profound and simple wisdom. It will stir life in others.
Bring Me to the forefront of your life.
Strip away all busyness and distraction.
Give Me the place of honor in your life.
Give Me the best, the first fruits.
You are effective.
You are an arrow in My hand.
You are enough, and when we walk together, what can be against us? You were born to overcome. Waves of My Spirit, are washing over you, refreshing and filling every dry place...only fullness.

Day 78

My Child...

I am the lifter of your head.
Fix your eyes on Me, the author and perfecter of your faith.
Do not carry things that are not meant for you to bear.
You were created for a purpose, minister to Me.
From there, go...and all shall happen.
I shall restore and repair all the breaches in your life, in your mind, and in your emotions.

My spirit ministers to you...use that to go forth by My Spirit to do all things, in all situations.
Ministering spirits are all around.
Go in the power and the strength that I have given you.
Do not look to others to measure or judge what I am doing in your life. When you surrender, you are an arrow in My hand, effective and precise...accomplishing what I have sent you out to do.
As you pray, I am removing walls and blocks.
The path is being cleared.
Press in.

Day 79

My Child...

Great joy is part of your inheritance.
It is a source of strength for you.
The world is perplexed watching you endure difficult situations with love, peace, and joy. The world can't imagine why you are not falling apart or breaking under the pressure.

Within you is a deep reservoir that never runs dry.
Your confidence in Me translates into every area of your life...
it is strength...it is health to your bones.
I am your life-giving vine, draw your life from Me.
The world cannot perceive it because when you are connected to the Word, and draw your life from the Word, it brings death to every worldly thing.

Don't be confused when people come against you.
Understand they are drawing from death and passing death on.
But you are a life-giver with your life and with your tongue.
You are My child imitating your Father.
I make My face shine upon you, and I am gracious to you.
I lift My countenance to you.
I give you peace and you reflect Me.

Day 80

My Child...

You are free and uninhibited to seek Me.
Every chain has been broken...so rise, shake off the dust, and come sit in the place of honor I have for you.
Remove the chains of slavery from your neck.
As I said upon the cross, My work is finished,
and I am now seated with My Father.

I gave you the keys.
Don't stay a slave from that which you have been freed.
An animal once caged and enchained will remain,
even though he has been loosed from his chains.

What will you do with what I have given you?
Will you plant and sow?
Will you reap, harvest, and bless?
It is your destiny to do good...to worship Me in spirit and truth.
You lack nothing. You live in fullness, plenty, and abundance.
You, My child, are My rich and glorious inheritance.
I redeemed you for such a time as this.

Day 81

My Child...

You must be perfected in My love.
Loving Me and loving others must be at the forefront of your heart and mind. I will make your heart burn for the unloved and the lost.
I will put My words in your mouth for them, and they will be drawn to Me through you.
Ask for divine appointments.
I give you eyes to see and ears to hear what they are really saying... not the words that are coming out of their mouths, but what is in their hearts and their deep longings.

You must walk in wholeness and fullness to do this.
Allow Me to heal any wounds and doubts you have.
From that place, you will move.
Put My Word in your heart.
Eat it, meditate on it, and it will be life for you.
Living water, bubbling up, and overflowing.
The fruit that comes from that act will be immeasurable, beloved.

Day 82

My Child...

My Word is truth.
It must become more real and trustworthy than any tangible thing.
If My Word lives in you,
it will become a real substance when mixed with your faith.
Trust it.
Make a demand on My Word. Your faith and belief in My Word move Me to move for you, beloved. My Word must overshadow every circumstance in your life.

By My Spirit you are led into all truth.
Learn to be a good receiver like an innocent child who receives with great joy. This world brings trouble, but with Me you overcome. You become more...
you are expanded and perfected in Me.
Don't be downcast when problems arise.
Look at them as opportunities to grow in trust, surrender, grace, and perfection. What do you have to fear or dread? What can happen? Don't fear, for it can only kill the body.
Oh death, where is your sting? I overcame the grave.

You will never cease to exist.
You will live forever with Me, so do not fear, My child.
Decide in your heart this day whom you will serve.
It will cost you everything, but what you give will be given back, pressed down, shaken together, and running over.
You can never outgive Me.
My desire is to bless you,
and I take such pleasure in you.

Day 83

My Child...

Keep your child-like innocence and wonder.
Feel excitement and joy.
Love much and laugh greatly.
I removed burdens from your neck.
Gentle, loving, and kind is how you are known in heaven.
I showed you the example, for I am gentle and humble of heart.
The world will not see or acknowledge you for the value and worth
I have assigned to you. You must live from a place of knowing you
are greatly loved and that you may love greatly.

Build and encourage the lives of My people.
The Spirit is where you speak from. That is the real you.
Speak to the gift and call forth the treasures I have placed in
people. Activate. Yes, activate the life in people.
The living water flows out of you,
and it will bring the dead things back to life.
Sit in My presence and I will continue to fill you. You lack nothing.
You are equipped for every good work.
Believe My Word over everything in this natural world.

Day 84

My Child...

I am the beginning and the end.
I created all things for a specific purpose.
Rest in Me...abide in Me...and I will direct your life.
No good thing do I withhold from the one who walks upright before Me. I reward those who diligently seek Me.
Allow yourself to be delighted by Me and consumed by Me.

Life with Me is a delight.
It is filled with joy and fulfillment.
When you walk in what I have created you for,
there is fullness of joy.
I never change.
I am the same yesterday, today, and forever.
Fix yourself on Me.
Know that you are on a sure foundation and go in that assurance.
Go with boldness and strength to the destiny I called you.

Day 85

My Child...

In a wealthy man's home, some utensils are made of gold and silver, and some are made of wood and clay. The expensive utensils are used for special occasions, and the lesser for everyday use.
If you keep yourself pure you will be My special treasure, used for honorable purposes. Your life will be clean, and you will be ready for your Master to use you for every good work.

Pursue righteous living, faithfulness, love, and peace.
Enjoy companionship with those who call on Me with pure hearts.
Live your life without entanglements that wrap you up and draw you away. Meditate and look at your life to see the entanglements.

What habits draw you away and steal your time, energy, and joy?
I set you in freedom from them all.
The chains are broken, the blinders are removed.
Your ways may seem to be right in your own eyes, but My ways are not your ways, and My thoughts are not your thoughts.
Come up to My higher thoughts and ways.
Be willing to step away from the familiar and the worldly.

Day 86

My Child...

What is in your heart and what you are dreaming of?
It is My desire to fulfill your dreams and your heart's desire.
You must understand that you are a beloved child. Your value
and worth are so great that Jesus gave His very life for you.
He left the splendors of heaven for you to be reconciled to Me.

The world will not recognize your value.
The enemy will attack your identity every time.
You must be rooted in My love and your identity rooted in Me.
You must have My holy fire. You must burn with My holy fire.
It is not by your power or strength, but by My Spirit.
Nothing will be impossible, all things are possible with Me.
The spirit of grace and the spirit of glory come upon you.
Goodness and mercy are with you all the days of your life.

Day 87

My Child...

My peace I have given you.
Not as the world gives do I give...rest in Me.
When the world brings worries and cares, simply be still and know that I am your God. Be still and rest in Me and see what I will do for you. I hear your heart, I hear your desires. I say all is well. Trust in Me and allow the joy from your spirit to well up and overflow. Lift up your face to Me. I have created you for good works. You are a redemptive fire to others.

Once you truly believe and understand that you are greatly loved and valued, move from that place, you will not fail. You will succeed as you live and move, knowing you have your being in Me. There is no struggle in Me, only *"Yes, and Amen," "Yes, and Amen."* My anointing oil pours forth over you and your life. The oil of gladness is upon you.

Not in your strength or power,
but by My Spirit will you accomplish, understand, and receive.
I receive you.
I rejoice over you.
I delight in you.
Seek Me for direction and the specific plan for your life.
Be quiet before Me and wait.
Be willing to wait until you hear.
I am here, so trust Me to take you through your process,
for I am perfecting you.

Day 88

My Child...

How can two walk together unless they agree?
Give My Spirit permission and freedom to work in your life.
Think partnership. Think, yoked together.
Your permission and surrender are needed.
You are free, beloved. Freedom in your mind, freedom from past hurts, freedom from illness. Free to have overflowing joy.
Free in the Spirit. There can be no doubting...just trust and faith.

Chains are breaking.
There is beauty for ashes...the joy and gladness overflowing.
Living water flows from your belly bringing the dead things back to life. Resurrection power flows through you. You are a life-giving being. You are My child and that is from Me.
Life from your spirit, life from your mouth.
Speak life into yourself and others.

I speak over you and sing over you. I have dreams for you.
You are complete in Me and there is fullness in My presence.
Go out in that fullness. Protect it.
Don't allow your identity to be diminished by this world.
You are in My hand and cannot be snatched away.
You are secure in Me.
I am gentle and lowly in heart, and you will find rest with Me.

Day 89

My Child...

My heart is full when I think of you.
The journey can seem long but when you put Me first,
we move swiftly and discover much together.
But time and time again, something happens, and your attention,
focus, and time is taken away from Me.
As you mature in Me, distractions will happen less and less...
you will be less shaken and pulled away.

You are a pacesetter, beloved.
The more you trust Me, the more I can help you.
I will answer your cry for help every time you pray.
I am here with the answers to show you the way.
I make your paths straight and your plans succeed. The plans
I have for you will require you to be whole, healed, and free.
I'm pouring out fullness upon you.
You lack nothing, beloved.

Day 90

My Child...

Don't be content to stay hidden in the background.
When My Spirit moves, it empowers and gives you revelation and words of wisdom. Do not hide that light. Speak it out with boldness and thankfulness that you are a vessel, being useful to the Master. For My righteous ones are as bold as lions. Be assured that I am working in you and through you.

Carry no offense.
Choose the fruit of the Spirit, for when you choose the fruit of Satan it is always the work of the flesh. (Galatians 5:19)
You are My child. Imitate Me.
For I cause the sun to shine on both the evil and good.
I send the rain on the just and unjust alike. (Matthew 5:45)
Beloved, you will encounter troubles, but stay the course.
Walk and run into spiritual maturity.
Allow Me to heal every wound and carry every burden.

Be a friend who is closer than a brother.
I send you out into the harvest. Lay aside all the entanglements.
Run with joy, fullness, and the lightness of My yoke.
So much becomes entangled, but it should not be like this.

Day 91

My Child...

My freedom is upon you.
You are free to dream and step out by the leading of My Spirit.
Have boldness and be assured when it comes to things of the Spirit.
You were created for such a time as this.
Ask and keep on asking. Open your mouth wide and I will fill it.
I desire to show you the mysteries...to give you revelation and the keys to every victory. Have no hesitation about what I want to give you and where I want to take you.

Be a good receiver where I am concerned.
I am good and I love to give good things to My children.
I give to those who diligently seek Me.
As this heavenly prayer goes forth, a troop of angels is being sent out. Do not listen to the voice of the enemy who wants to keep you in a small place...a place of doubt and lack.

I have given you Dunamis power.
Like dynamite exploding, it is yoke-breaking power.
I give you fresh anointing oil.
Showers of blessings are all around you.
I want you to have a tangible, life-giving relationship with Me...
not just a touch here and there, but constant and consistent.
I am looking for those to whom I can show myself strong on their behalf, whose hearts are completely loyal to Me. Heavy anointing will rest upon you...heavy anointing for every good work.

Day 92

My Child...

Walk with Me.
I must be first in your heart and life.
I will add everything and there will be no sorrow with it.
All distance that you are feeling is a lack of trust in Me.

Day 93

My Child...

I am your great reward.
Press into Me for the breakthrough.
I have you and hold you secure.
No other thing can have a hold on you.
No other thing can have a hold on you.
Look to Me.
I will give you victory in whatever situation and circumstance
you are walking through. You need to break through.
Trust in Me and do not take your eyes off Me.

You are being purified by fire and you will come out
as pure gold with all the dross and impurities removed.
Have joy and assurance through this process.
It has purpose and I will work it all out for your good.
Do not despise the process.

Guard your mouth and speak that which edifies the listeners.
Call out the good in others.
Speak your direction and heart's desire,
not your current circumstances.
This is life to you.

You have freedom within the pleasant boundaries
I have set for you.
I want you to have ears to hear, eyes to see,
and sensitivity to the Spirit realm and My heart.
I will fill your mouth with words to speak.
I will give you revelation and the ability to guide My people.
Do not doubt.
Your identity comes from Me and what I have said about you,
not from things that are here today and gone tomorrow.

Day 94

My Child...

You are seated with Me in the heavenly realm.
You operate in two realms.
Let your mind be set on things above.
Arise, arise. I lift you out of the muck and mire.
Trust in Me, allow Me to have first place in your heart and mind.
No eye has seen, no ear has heard the mighty works and plans I have for your life.

I release you from every stronghold, lie, and weakness.
Seek My face.
In My presence there is fullness of joy.
I have dreams for you.
I have goodness for you to walk in every day.
Observe the things that have a hold on your life.
Renounce the agreement you have come into with them and allow My Spirit to come and fill the space those things have occupied.

Day 95

My Child...

There is grace upon you.
Grace for every good work and every situation.
Grace draws those around you into the Kingdom realm,
those who are present with My children.
Your feet are planted firmly on the rock of Jesus.
Your emotions are planted on that rock,
and everything comes through the rock.
The rock absorbs the shock and sting, so you are not easily moved.
That is why your emotions are not tossed back and forth, to and fro, like the waves of the ocean.

You are seated with Me in the heavenly realm.
All the answers are there,
so don't be tempted to look back and lament or question.
That is not from Me. I say,
"Look this way. Look at what I have said and walk this way."
Trust Me for every detail and to perfect you in love.
I love to see you joyful in Me and in your life.
Keep joy in the forefront.
Laugh and be lighthearted,
for My yoke is easy and My burden is light.
I release you from every entanglement and burden.

My Word is alive and active. Eat My Word.
Find yourself within the pages of it as one of My devoted disciples.
The entrance of My Word brings light.
Relax in Me...rest in Me.
My anointing breaks the yoke.
I am a yoke breaker and I set you free.
You are under My anointing to set others free.
Break through, break through.

Day 96

My Child...

I am speaking a declaration over you.
My truth be revealed.
In whatever way you are veiled or obscured, I remove it right now.
I remove every blinder and blind spot, the veil has been torn.

Draw near to Me, beloved.
Lay back. Recline on My chest and feel My heartbeat for you.
I have so much for you, so be quick to lay aside all offenses and be quick to forgive.
I want to touch those wounds and bring healing and restoration.
I want to restore you back to wholeness, fullness, and overflowing with My love and joy for you.

Day 97

My Child...

All things are in My hands, beloved.
Hear Me, all things are in My hands.
You must grasp the revelation of My love for you.
The depth, width, height, and intensity.
There is nothing I hold back from you.
I give you everything when you accept that you are My beloved,
My desire. There will be a breakthrough...a quickening...
an acceleration of your destiny in Me.

I am love and you must become a good receiver of My love for you.
In Me, there is no lack...only abundance.
No confusion...only a sound mind.
No unworthiness.
I see you as I created you.
You turned out exactly as I planned for you.
You were created to love Me and be loved by Me.
Walk in this, beloved.
Meditate on Me and My great love for you.

Day 98

My Child...

The one who sees the invisible will do the impossible.
Each time the King of Syria came against Israel,
the plan of attack was thwarted. (2 Kings 6:8)
This is no coincidence.
It was not in the natural but by the Spirit.

The same Spirit that raised Jesus from the dead will also give life to your mortal body. Through the same Spirit who lives in you, I want to use you to thwart the plans of your enemies, and for individuals and masses to have blinders removed...to confuse the enemy...
to bring My Kingdom to every area.

Day 99

My Child...

I desire to pour out such abundance for you.
You have not because you ask not.
What would you ask Me for if you had no limitations,
if the sky was the limit? Think about that, My child.
I have put you here for such a time as this.
This is your time to rise above your circumstances.
Come up to My higher thoughts.
Come up to My higher ways.
Let your heart not be troubled.
Cast all your cares upon Me, for I care for you so deeply...
so passionately...so completely.

You are a joy to Me.
Allow Me to touch every area in your life that is not in alignment with Me or My Word. When you choose to do this, an acceleration will happen. Pray for My grace in this area.
When Peter denied Me, he had to allow Me to touch that wound in him and be restored before he could move in Me again in fullness.
Be in fullness, My child.

Day 100

My Child ...

Knit your heart to Me, beloved.
Attach...attach. We must be interwoven.
Do not try to make sense of what is going on in the natural.
My Word brings clarity. My Word is absolute truth.
That is your starting place for everything.
Put My Word in your heart.
It will go down and produce a crop.
It will produce fruit.
Eat My word...feast on it.
It is life to you. It is goodness to you.

Day 101

My Child...

I want you to walk in the fullness of My joy.
There is something that is warring against this joy.
It is your expectations.
Let go of how you think situations should look and feel.
Trust in Me.
Hope in Me...
not in your will, but My will in your life,
which will surpass your wildest dreams and thoughts.

Your valley of tears has ended.
In heaven, there is no sadness, pain, or tears.
On earth as it is in heaven, beloved.
On earth, as it is in heaven.

You have the mind of My beloved son, Jesus.
As He is, so are you.
As you stand on this earth for Me, do it with joy.
Count it all joy as you stand in the gap for your loved ones.
Understand you are a victor.
Stand as one who has already won.

Again, I say to you, let go of every expectation,
release thoughts that something does not feel right.
Simply stand. Be faithful and have joy.
Watch Me. Watch what I will do for you, My faithful one.
Trust Me with the outcome of every one of your situations.

Day 102

My Child...

There is no struggle in Me.
There is freedom and fullness.
There is permission granted.
I grant you grace to rise above all the circumstances you are facing.
I love your confidence and faith in Me.
I will never leave you or forsake you. You are My beloved child.

I am perfecting you. Talk to Me...
bring your bad news,
and I will turn it into good for My Kingdom.
I give beauty for ashes, joy for despair,
and strength for weakness...
it is My divine exchange.
You will run and not grow weary. You will walk and not faint.

Day 103

My Child...

Opposition attaches to whatever you have not surrendered to Me. Begin to declare over your life those things you desire but do not yet have. Your faith brings your hopes into reality, and they become the foundation needed to acquire the things you long for. It is all the evidence needed to prove that which is still unseen.

There is no struggle in Me.
This life is filled with joy.
As you learn how to walk in the fruit of the Spirit,
your everyday life is your joy.
It will give you the grace to overcome.

The wise in heart are called discerning.
Speaking sweet and gracious words to others promotes instruction. Wisdom is a deep well of understanding within you. It is a fountain of life to benefit others.
However, do not cast your pearls before swine...it is senseless to instruct a fool. The heart of the wise teaches his mouth and adds learning to his lips.
Gracious, beautiful, life-giving words release sweetness to our souls and healing to our bones.

Day 104

My Child...

Jesus was the bread that came down from heaven.
Eat My Word. Put My Word before your eyes and ears...be
transformed. As you continually meditate on My word, you will
think differently. Your life and world will be framed by My Word.
I know you want to change.

Eat My Word and meditate on it...this is your key.
It will plant a seed in you that will create a substance and grow.
In that place your questions will be answered.
There is only peace, joy, and righteousness.
As your mind stays fixed on Me and My word,
allow it to root out every wrong belief and false doctrine.
People will look at you and see glimpses of My glory in your face.
Strengthen your inward spirit man. You are a spirit being and when
you are led by anything else, it is out of order and will bring conflict.

Day 105

My Child...

My sheep hear My voice. I am always speaking.
Put yourself in a position to hear Me.
My voice must be allowed to be prominent in your life.
Quiet. Quiet yourself and be still in My presence.

Be like Jesus,
in whom the enemy could not find a place to hook His flesh.
Be holy, for I am holy. As you sojourn on this earth,
look to Me to fulfill every area, every emotion, and every need.
I know your needs and I love to lavish you with every good and perfect gift.

I give you My peace.
My peace covers and envelops every issue...
your racing mind, your broken heart,
and the realization that you will not fall short in any area.
Be free to lose your life for My sake,
only then will you gain everything.
My grace is there for you.
It is necessary for this life.
Grace and peace be with you...grace and peace.
I give grace for every good work...grace over the words you speak.

Day 106

My Child...

I am so pleased when you seek My face. I will be found by you.
I have great joy when you press into Me. I am your great reward.
Diligently seek Me...listen for My voice. Meditate on My Word and the prophetic words given by My prophets.
Study My Kingdom. It is yours to carry in this realm.
I am glorified by your life and your well-being...by your living well and prospering. I am good and there are so many experiences I want you to have. Encounter the joy I have all around you.

Rejoice in your salvation. Rejoice in your eternal life.
You must resist the things that want to pull down your heart and soul. Resist the hooks and traps set by the enemy.
I will show you the path I have for you.
My path is filled with peace and answers.
Clarity and partnership come with My Kingdom.
Release all your expectations. My ways are higher.
My plans and purposes look very different.
Do not think you know what My way will look like.
That is why you follow your good shepherd.
I will lead you into everything.
I have no limits, everything is Mine.

Day 107

My Child...

Relax, I am here.
Rest in Me for I have all things under My watchful eye.
The floodgates are open. Be drenched in the flowing living water.
Guard your heart and allow My presence to soften and tenderize your heart for Me. I want you extremely sensitive to My voice and Spirit. I want you as a little child.

Allow Me to minister to you, child, as your loving Father desires.
This life cannot be lived well without dependence upon My Spirit.
I am your deep well, your strong tower, and your rock.
I am the restorer and the repairer of every breach in your life.
I can make all things new. Nothing is ever too hard for Me, just believe. Love much and forgive everyone.

Your joy is restored. I speak fullness to you, My child. Fullness.
I am your never-ending supply. I am thinking of you.
My eye is watching you. Choose well, beloved.
Choose My Kingdom. Choose love, joy, peace, and patience.
Choose self-control and long-suffering.
You are My child.
Follow Me and walk like Me.

Day 108

My Child...

My eyes see you. I am delighted by you, My child.
I know you. I know everything about you.
There is no part of you that is hidden from Me.
I understand you even better than you understand yourself.
I see your needs and I desire to bring you into fullness.

You are My ambassador, bringing My will and My plans on earth as it is in heaven. You live and move and have your being in Me.
You live in two realms. You are a spirit being.
I am speaking and directing your spirit.

Ask and keep asking.
My timing is different than yours.
Trust My timing for your life.
Things will happen.
Things will move.
Do not grow weary.

Day 109

My Child...

You are free. I have given you such freedom in Me, beloved.
I release you into the fullness of your destiny.
Call it out...speak it forth. Do not grow weary. Hold fast.
Press in...the breakthrough is at hand.

I am jealous for you. I desire intimacy with you.
Be a devoted lover to Me. My thoughts toward you are endless.
Come up to My higher thoughts and be in agreement with My thoughts about you. You were created for good.
You were created for relationship with Me.
Devotion to Me is good for you.
You are prepared for every good work.
You will not fail or fall short.
Take care and nurture your spirit.
Eat My Word.
Study and meditate.

Day 110

My Child...

I created the heavens and earth.
As long as they endure, even the smallest detail will by no means pass from the law until all is fulfilled. You are the burnt offering. You are the living sacrifice on the brazen altar.

I look and see into your heart. I look at your intentions.
I desire pure worshipers...purity in heart and love.
Purity in devotion to Me. Do not be deceived.
I will not be mocked.

For what you sow you will reap.
It may look like the wicked have their way and prosper,
but it is not so. Do not look to them longingly or with envy.
Their throats are open graves, and they are in the snare.
Their cleverness has trapped them.
Look with joy to My Kingdom. Seek and you will find.
Overflowing fullness is your inheritance and birthright as the beloved. I am with you. I want to redeem the time in your life.

Day 111

My Child...

My words are in your mouth. Speak the words of life and spirit.
I receive every effort you make and every step you take
for My kingdom. I have a high calling on your life.
There is grace present for every good work.
I make the way and I make your path straight.
I create paths in the wilderness and a way when there is no way.
Look straight ahead. Forge ahead on the path of the narrow way.

I want to give you the revelation of My kingdom.
The infinite, abundant, strategic Kingdom.
You must be loosed from ties that bind and distract you.
Come into a Kingdom mindset...Kingdom living.
Find your strength in Me, strength in your thinking.
I remove all weakness in the mind and thoughts.

Arise and take the place I purchased for you.
You are precious and valuable to Me. The price paid for you was
great and costly...not paid for with perishable things like gold or
silver but with the precious blood of Jesus, My son.
He completed His work and ran His race.
Look to him and run your race.
Each day is a gift. Go in the might I have given you.
Trust that I have equipped you for the assignment I have given you.

Day 112

My Child...

I am with you. You are never alone so do not fear.
Believe in your good future and in My good plans for your life.
Live everyday under the wings of My goodness and grace.
Allow My goodness to overtake you and change everything about you for good.

I am good and I love to be good to you.
I want you to have a revelation of My goodness and I want you to see and experience it daily.
I want you to have the fullness of My kingdom now.
It can be just as real and tangible as touching your kitchen table.
I give you eyes to see, ears to hear, and a heart to perceive.
There is no lack with Me. There is fullness and plenty.

I will order your steps and you will have the victory in Me.
I am freeing the constraints of your mind to allow you to dream big.
See yourself through My eyes...for a vision of your future.
I have put things in your heart that need to be birthed and allowed to manifest. Be bold. I have given you everything you need.

Day 113

My Child...

I am the lifter of your head. I lift the burden off your neck.
I send My angels to encamp around those who fear Me.
They will be delivered with great victory. (Psalm 34:7)
I know everything about you. I am thinking of you every
moment and I am aware of your every need.

Come to Me for I desire such closeness and intimacy.
I am your great reward. I am your victor and banner.
You must step out and be willing to risk all to believe Me.
Your faith will cost you...consider the cost.
Taste and see that I am good. Settle every doubt in your heart
that says otherwise. The enemy does not speak truth but lies.
Close the door to every place in your life he has access to.

Because you can receive lies and truth into your heart,
you must make the choice to be devoted to one and not the other.
I am not pleased with double mindedness. Faith pleases Me.
I am not pleased with lukewarmness.
I love zeal and passion for My Kingdom.
I do not like partial worship...
I love true worshipers who fully worship Me in spirit and in truth.
Let the truth come out of your heart beloved.
Look with eyes wide open, examine your heart.

Day 114

(From the author: I had a vision of waves washing over us.)

My Child...

Each day I pour My unfailing love upon you.
I give you life...My life surges in you.
My Spirit dwells in you, giving you Dunamis power, wisdom, fullness, hope, and joy. Your spirit must lead you.
You must choose to surrender and submit your lives.

By My design, we partner and work together in unity.
Hear and obey...you are a spirit being and I want to reveal mysteries to those who are Spirit led. Deny yourself.
Take up your cross and follow Me...
I will direct your path and order your steps.
I am always speaking. Hear Me...be still and hear Me.
Do not be reactors to situations. Respond to Me and My Kingdom, watching for My cues and direction.

Day 115

My Child...

I am El Shaddai, your all-sufficient one.
Lay back and rest upon My chest.
I know...I understand. You are never alone.
You are not a forsaken one.
I am with you always, even to the very end of the age.
You are the redeemed...the chosen. Look to your life...
have eyes to see the entanglements the enemy uses to keep you busy, tired, frustrated, and in a small place.
By My Spirit and grace, you can overcome the entanglements. Your whole heart, soul, and spirit are needed for My kingdom purposes.

As He is, so are you. He was about His Father's business so you should be about your Father's business too.
Open your mouth wide...I will fill it with my Word.
Speak forth My Word. Bring forth life by your words.
The enemy is the god of this world,
which means he has access to you because you are in this domain.
You are a spirit being and you must live out of your spirit, so the voice of the Holy Spirit comes forth loud and clear.
This is not a strange thing so don't be confused.
You are in the world but not of it.
I have called you and marked you.
You are Mine...My ambassador.
Ask Me for what you need. Seek Me for what you desire. Knock and keep knocking, for it will all be revealed and come to light.

Day 116

My Child...

Take My yoke upon you. Put your hand in My hand.
Agree with Me and let's walk together. Be one spirit with the Holy Spirit. Go deep...for only My Spirit knows the depths of My heart.
I will teach you all things.
Press in, for the breakthrough is there.
I want to flood you with the light of My glory.
I am near to you.
I broke every chain.
I removed every curse.

Day 117

My Child...

Open your heart to receive My correction.
I discipline and correct My beloved children.
This too can be a joyful process as you understand the good fruit you will produce...fruit that will last and reproduce.
I know you want to be different and for change to come.
Be of good cheer for I have overcome in all those areas.
My spirit will show you through...and you will come out on the other side just as pure gold comes out of the purifying fire with all impurities and dross removed.

When you confessed Me as your Lord and Savior, you received My DNA. My very Spirit dwells in you and you are equipped for every good work I have prepared for you.
You have everything you need for this life and godliness.
Your quality of life in the Spirit is so important to Me.
I want the abundant life for you. I love to hear you laugh as you overcome by My goodness for you. I have a high place for you.
Don't worry if you feel as if you are living below it, for that is where My correction and discipline is needed.

Be a good receiver.
Don't be offended...open your heart to receive,
knowing it is out of love.
Allow Me to put My finger on the wound,
for I am your repairer and restorer.
Let's dream about your life together.
I breathe life into you, and I breathe upon those things that you thought were a distant past. They are alive again.

...continued.

The world rejected Me,
and because you are in Me, it will reject you too.
If you are looking for validation in this world, you will not get it.
If you find some acceptance, it will come at a high cost because
the enemy will want payback. You can only be truly known
by the Spirit. That is your true DNA...the true you.
Through My Spirit, I have equipped you for every situation...
to be a warrior, leader, son or daughter, brother or sister,
friend, and encourager.

Day 118

My Child...

Stay close to Me. Let there be no distance between us.
For you must live, move, and have your being in Me
Time is short...make the most of your days for they are fleeting.
Shake off the dust...the bands that hold you have been cut.
Run and don't grow weary. Do good to all.
Be known by your love and generosity.
I see everything, beloved...
every tear, every small act of love and kindness...
everything prompted by your faith.

My eye is upon you, and I am near. You are the light in this
world...a flame burning bright with holy fire and passion.
Zeal for My house must consume you, beloved.
Your zeal and love please Me.
Stay close to Me. Let there be no distance between us,
for from Me you can do nothing.
I long to give you your heart's desire for My glory.
I want to fulfill your longings.
I want you to enjoy life and fellowship with Me and others.
Unity, love, joy, and peace are your inheritance and birthright.

Don't you know there is no lack with Me?
Don't you know perfect love casts out all fear?
I want you to know what is available to you.
Read My Word. Stay very close to Me.
I cover you in the shadow of My wings.

Day 119

My Child...

Tell Me your burdens and blocks,
for My desire is to remove them for you.
I have already removed them in the spirit,
but I am with you as you walk through them in the natural.
I take your hand in My hand so we can walk together toward victory.
You have freedom. You have permission.
I say to you, *"Yes, and Amen." "Yes, and Amen."*
I am always speaking to you...praying over you...singing over you.

There is a deep reservoir available to you.
It is filled with wisdom, knowledge, and revelation.
You can access this reservoir in the spirit realm at any time you desire. I am unlimited and eternal.
The world and all its fullness are Mine.
There is grace for each situation.
Step out...move...and that reservoir will flow.
In the book of John, Jesus told the woman at the well, *"If you only knew what I have to give you, you would ask Me for a drink and never thirst again."*

Day 120

My Child...

He who the son sets free is free indeed.
I want to touch every area of your life,
especially the areas where you already feel victorious.
Allow Me to take you to a deeper level to bring more freedom and revelation. Understand, it is not by your might, nor by your power, but by My Spirit.

I understand and see in your heart.
When we are yoked together, we can do all things.
Do not run ahead and do things in your own power and wisdom, then tell Me about it afterward.
Take every step, every breath, every act, and every decision together with Me.

Jesus only did what He saw Me doing.
You have to make the choice whether you will surrender it all.
What needs to be done will take surrender.
You were bought at a high price. Your life is no longer your own...you are either a slave to sin or a slave to righteousness as a son or daughter. Allow Me to uncover what I have placed in you. Allow My Spirit to show you all the treasures in and around you.
I want to show you great things, beloved.
I want more freedom for you.

Day 121

My Child...

I am gentle and humble in heart. Be at rest in Me, beloved.
There are two distinct kingdoms and each bear different fruits.
What you plant, you will reap, so examine yourself.
Let love be your motivation for all things.
I have freed you from your bondage, so do not go back into slavery.
Build one another up in the faith. Encourage one another and spur each other on to do good works.
I am gentle, so be gentle on yourself and be gentle with others.

Enjoy the journey.
Let My joy come upon you.
Enjoy learning. Laugh and smile, for I smile over you.
You have everything you need. You are simply learning how to access and use what I have given you. Work with My Spirit and the gifts will spring forth and blossom beautifully in My time.
Be patient with yourself.
Taste and see I am good. Be good to yourself.
Start inwardly at first, then it will flow outwardly to others.

Day 122

My Child...

My Kingdom is light and in it, there is no darkness.
The weightiness of glory is feather-light and breaks chains.
Pray over situations. Bring the Kingdom's power over and around it. The anointing covers, spreads, and smears.
What you intercede for is heard and responded to.
Be assured of this. Intercession is gold and of great value.
Do not allow yourself to stumble over the expectation of what you think the timing or results of your prayers should be.

I am the lifter of your head.
My love for you is difficult for you to understand.
I give you the revelation of My love, for I have held nothing back from you. I gave you My only begotten Son.
He made the way because I want fellowship with you, My bride, prepared without spot or wrinkle. I see you that way.

You are My beloved one. I see you how I created you...the true you.
I see your spirit. My eye is upon you. Your eyes see the flaws,
but I don't see as you do. My eye goes to the truth.
I see the motivation of your heart.
I see your struggles and I am with you through everything.
I see when you weep. I rejoice when you rejoice.
When you call, I say *"Lo, I am here."* I will not let your foot slip.
I am good and My goodness is all around you.
Time is in My hand...your time is in My hand.
Be willing to lose everything for Me. Release everything to Me...watch and see what I will do for you.

Day 123

My Child...

The areas in which you feel sufficient are the very places I desire to touch and give you greater victory.
I want you to learn and understand how to be a good steward of the things you have and of the gifts I have placed in you.
Give of yourself generously.
Hold nothing back.

Day 124

My Child...

You are My sent one.
Hear My voice, then act, beloved.
My Kingdom requires great love, action, and vision by My Spirit.
There is great beauty...the beauty of My holiness.
I want to give you a revelation of My holiness.
I want to give you inventions...clever ideas for the good of humanity. I give you the ability and grace to pierce and infiltrate areas that are considered difficult to enter.

Today is your day. Now is the appointed time, beloved.
Who can I use? Who will go?
Give Me your willing heart...surrender to Me.
My righteous ones are as bold as lions. They do not shrink back.
We take ground. We shine light on darkness.
We give hope to those in despair. See it in your heart.
Picture it...speak it...go forth and take ground.

Day 125

My Child...

Have eyes to see those I have placed around you to receive your kindness, counsel, and encouragement.
Build up My kingdom by loving My sheep.
My kingdom is simple. Receive it as a child.
Be in awe and wonder over My kingdom.
When you follow Jesus, you receive everything.

Be known by the fruit of the Spirit.
Allow them to pour through your life.
There are other works that won't remain.
They will be burned up with fire. What you do for My kingdom in love is good work that will remain and bear lasting fruit.
You shall be called a minister of God.

Day 126

My Child...

I am timely I send the rain in its time.
I protect you from harm and send provision and goods.
My tender love is blended into everything I do.
I fill the sky with clouds that send showers to water the earth,
so the grass springs up on the mountains and fields. I blanket
the earth with glistening snow.
I speak a word and it all Melts away.
I speak My Word to you by My Spirit.
I give you life-giving instruction.

I enjoy My faith-filled ones.
I adorn the humble with beauty. I love to give them victory.
By My Spirit, I give you revelation that illuminates and ignites truth.
Take My Word and eat it...devour it...it is your very life.
It is a life-producing treasure for you.
Who among you wants to be wise?
Speak My Word and allow it to come forth.
My life-giving words are the answer to all your questions.

Day 127

My Child...

My way is so broad for you, beloved.
We can do all things together. Align with Me...join your spirit with My Spirit...the entry point to the wide and broad place.
The entry of My Word brings light and revelation to you.
I have this beautiful, bountiful banquet set for you.
Come...dine and fellowship with Me.

Receive all things from My hand.
The finest tastes and the most beautiful aromas are all around, perfuming the air of our fellowship. There is such joy and pleasure in our fellowship together. Your adoring love is so joyous to Me.
I love it when you worship Me in fullness...unashamed.
My spirit will lead you into all My goodness.
Bask in the light and drink in the fullness of life in the Spirit.
The broad places are deep, wide, high, and expansive.
The atmosphere is thick with the Spirit.

Day 128

My Child...

My Kingdom takes you above this natural realm...a higher realm, vision, and mindset. You are above the problems and issues of this world with the vantage point I have appointed for you.
When you are upset, worried, and frustrated, it is because you have come down to this level. I have provided all you need to stay with Me in the heavenly realm. Keep your eyes on things above.

I see your needs, I see all things. Ask for what you desire.
I am your provider...your great reward.
I am a covering for you. I go before you and behind you.
I surround you. Do not fear, for I am with you.

You are a joy to Me and in you,
My Spirit lives and has expression in this world.
Allow the spirit to have His way.
I am the author of your faith.
I am the finisher of your faith.
I am the beginning and the end.
I have called you up. I have called you to a higher realm.
Take My thoughts as your thoughts.
Take My Kingdom mindset that brings you to an emptying place.
Less of you, more of Me....infilling...infilling.

My hand is upon you. My grace and My glory are upon you.
You lack nothing...not one thing. All is available.
Everything is accessible to you.
Think blessing...think plentiful.
Let the mindset of being *"less than"* fade away.
It is planted by the enemy. It is a lie.

Allow My truth to wash over you and find its place in you.
I have made everything available to you, but you have to be the one to choose it. It is up to you how you live...above or below.
What you believe is up to you...truth or lies. It is your choice.
My covenant I will not break. (Psalm 89:34)

Day 129

My Child...

My grace is all around.
Love must always flow through you.
Forgiveness is a way of life. Bless and forgive.
Life will be rich in My kingdom with this on your heart and mind.

Day 130

My Child...

Above all, keep loving others earnestly.
My beloved child, put on a wrapping of compassion,
kindness, humility, meekness, and patience...bearing with others.
I give you My peace. Be at peace...it is always available.
Wash your face and put on joy and gladness. I want people to
see you in the light of My Kingdom on earth, as it is in Heaven.

Nothing you do in My name is a small thing. Lift your head.
Smile at others and give hope...the hope you have is so valuable.
I have given you a voice to speak goodness to others.
There is a season and time for every matter under Heaven.
(Ecclesiastes 3:1)

I give wisdom to the wise...
and knowledge to those who have understanding.
Whatever I do endures forever. (Ecclesiastes 3:14)
Nothing can be added to it, nor can anything be taken from it.

Day 131

My Child...

Go from glory to glory...victory to victory.
I initiate, draw, and call those who are Mine into obedience...
My fullness. As you obey Me, more will be revealed.
Sit at My feet...learn to be still in My presence.
Turn your eyes from people and put them on Me.
It is the doorway you need to enter in order to love unconditionally... to heal...to receive from Me. If you look to man or this world, it will lead to death.

My kingdom, My Spirit is life and peace to you.
Have joy through the emptying process. I will fill up those places.
I will repair and restore the breach in your life.
What are you looking for? What is your expectation?
Allow your hope to be in Me alone.
I will never disappoint you.
My love has been poured upon you...receive all I have for you.

Day 132

My Child...

I love obedience.
I came to serve, not to be served.
I gave the example of submission and servanthood.
No matter what your circumstances are or what is happening around you, stand firm in your calling.
Do not let this cup pass from you.
My gift was free, but it will cost you everything.
It is your choice to have leanness or fullness.

Purify yourself...set yourself apart.
Pray, fast, ask, and seek. Breakthrough is here...it is at hand.
The breaker is breaking through the blocks.
Strengthen and encourage yourself in Me.
I breathe on your circumstances, and I bring life.
Awaken and shake off the dust. Lose your life to Me.
Open your hand and your heart.
Let loose of expectations and you will gain everything.
Most assuredly I say to you, unless a grain of wheat falls to the ground and dies, it remains alone...
but if it dies, it produces much grain. (John 12:24)

Day 133

My Child...

Be holy, for I am holy.
When you follow My Son, you will receive everything.
Bring every hurt, disappointment, and heaviness to Me.
You must ask and allow Me in to heal those areas...the places that hold you back...the places that have stifled you.
Bring them all to Me. I can heal and restore.
Be willing to let go of everything the enemy can hook you with.

Come to Me in stillness as Daniel did when he knelt and prayed to Me throughout his day. Come to Me in fellowship as David did while tending his father's sheep. Come to Me in meekness as Moses did while shepherding his flocks.
Come...I am bidding you to come.
Come enter in. I am the doorway to your destiny.
Come...fulfillment will happen.
Place a high value on all that My kingdom has to give you.
Desire the kingdom, the gifts, and the fruits. Desire My fullness.

Day 134

My Child...

I do not conceal things from you...I reveal all things to you.
My Word contains all that you need here and now.
It has deep revelations and mysteries that the Holy Spirit can make known to you.
Eat My Word...it will be sweet as honey to you.
My words pierce and My words heal.
Truth is necessary for your path.
My Word of truth will illuminate your path. Read My Word.
Meditate on it to get it into your soul and spirit.
It will be planted down deep and bring forth good fruit.

Those who are Mine are bold as lions...fierce in their passion for Me. Hunger and thirst for Me, beloved.
I am life to you...a lifeline that can never be cut off or severed.
I am with you to the end of the age.
Shut down every distraction and clarity will come.
The enemy wants you to feel alone and cut off from everyone, but you are connected, grafted in, and joined into My family.
There are so many with you.
My comforting presence and power are with you.
I am delighted to be by your side.

Day 135

My Child...

My Word is a deep ocean of knowledge and wisdom.
Swim in the knowledge of Me.
Desire it...fan it into flames and make it your duty.
Seek it with all your heart.
This is your joyful part, beloved...seek and floodgates will open.
Even though you have My Spirit within you, as a foretaste of future glory, I long for your bodies to be released from sin and suffering. (Romans 8:23)

Eagerly wait to receive your full rights as My children, including your new bodies that I have promised. I have given you this hope.
You will have all I have spoken in My word, My child.
Wait patiently and confidently for My fullness.

Day 136

My Child...

There is a partnership in trusting and waiting.
Without that understanding, there's frustration and
disappointment. Be still in My presence. It is an active stillness.
Receive. You are learning by My Spirit.
Eating My Word brings light. Meditate and pray.
Wait patiently...through patience you inherit the promise.
Those who wait on Me inherit the land. (Romans 8:25)

Look forward to the things you don't have yet.
Wait patiently and confidently. Your confidence is in Me.
Believe I can and believe I will, beloved. Don't lose heart.
I love your heart towards Me.
Don't dismiss that because it is uncommon.

I have created you in a unique way, with characteristics I value.
Don't dismiss that. Appreciate and value all that I have put in you.
Sitting at My feet will activate all that is within you.
You were created in My image.

Day 137

My Child...

I am love. (1 John 4:8)
I have designed you with a great capacity to love.
The enemy's plan is to use hurts, struggles, and the trials you have been through to diminish this great capacity. Everything I have commanded you to do in this life can be fulfilled by love...loving Me and loving others. I am your great protector...your shield.
I stand beside you as a protective shield. (Psalm 121:5)
I gave you My armor so you can stand strong against the enemy's games. I sing songs of deliverance over you. (Psalm 32:7)

I will never leave you nor forsake you. (Deuteronomy 31:6)
I have overcome this world, and you are the victor.
You are in a battle and there are wounds.
The victory can be handed over by you to the enemy if you harden your heart and become cynical or jaded. The enemy also wins if you build walls of protection around yourself, walling yourself off.
I can heal everything. My arm is not too short.
Because I was wounded, you are healed.

Trust in Me...break down the walls and let love flow. Love covers a multitude of sins. The enemy cannot stand against love. Love binds everything together in perfect harmony. (Colossians 3:14)
Love is a weapon against the enemy.
Love tires and discourages him.
In My kingdom, it is the most important thing.
It is the key. It is the fulfillment.

Day 138

My Child...

How long will you waver between two masters?
Do not be discouraged.
That issue, the problem you can't seem to overcome...that thing
the devil taunts you with can be overcome with Me, beloved.
Arise, wash your face. I anoint you with the oil of gladness.
Arise and shine, for the light has dawned upon you...renewed hope.
Rejoice, again I say rejoice! Let the weak say I am strong.
Let the poor say I am rich.

Resurrection power is in you,
the same resurrection power that raised Jesus from the dead.
Be still in My presence. I breathe My breath of life upon you,
awakening you to My presence.
Stir up the gifts in you.
Arise and shine...shake off the dust. My holy fire engulfs you.
Don't look with natural eyes...take hold of that which I have for you.
In a moment, it can all change, and "suddenly" is here.
Nothing is impossible to him who believes.

So don't lose hope...the victory is here for you. It is finished.
You are the victor. Walk in that victory today.
You have the victor's crown. You are Mine.
I have placed My seal upon you, beloved.
We will walk together in unity and in fellowship for all time.

Day 139

My Child...

There is a season for everything. (Ecclesiastes 3:1-8)
A time to plant and a time to pluck what was planted.
A time to kill and a time to heal.
A time to embrace and a time to turn away.
A time to keep and a time to throw away.
I am speaking to you about the time to let loose, to pluck,
to turn away. I release you to let go and enter in,
without remorse or regret, to your new season...your new chapter.

Don't look back.
Put your hand to the plow and keep moving forward.
The enemy is in the "looking back."
The enemy is in the "what if's." Move in freedom.
I have things for you to do so don't get stuck in the
muck and mire of things that have been removed.

Day 140

My Child...

I have given you boundaries that fall in pleasant places.
You are under My care.
I guard all that is yours...all that is your inheritance.
I show you the way of life, I bring light to your path.
When you follow that path it leads to life.
The straight and narrow path will be broad for you.
Your foot will not stumble or slip.
Do not get carried away with the things of this world,
for I bore your grief and carried your sorrows.
I wipe every tear from your eyes. Your days of mourning are over.
Let your heart not be troubled. Believe in Me.
You know in part, but all things will become clear.
All things will be revealed to you.

You must surrender to the Spirit who is in you.
That is where everything flows from...the Living Water that brings
the dead things back to life. The Spirit gives life.
The Spirit is the one who guides you into all truth. He is the
revealer. The spirit is willing, the flesh is weak (Matthew 26:41)
Crucify your flesh daily, beloved. If you don't, your flesh will
strengthen daily because you are in the world...
it will overtake you and you will grow cold.

Burn with holy fire. Stir up the passion for My kingdom
and walk with like-minded people. Sharpen one another.
Be at peace and stop striving. Fellowship with the One who loves
you, who created you, and all other things will be added to your
life. It is not by your power or might, but by My Spirit, beloved.

Day 141

My Child...

Let your heart not be troubled.
I release you into the fullness of your blessing.
Now is the time of release. Release all bitterness.
Release all records of wrongs.
Release yourself into My hands...My care.
I work in you to will and to work for My good pleasure.
(Philippians 2:13)

Hold firmly to the Word of Life.
Live clean, innocent lives as My children.
Do everything without complaining and arguing.
Your faithful service is an offering to Me.
Work together with other believers...
work together with one mind and one purpose.

Day 142

My Child...

The process you're walking through can be a joy.
The enemy wants you to be a reactor to life and situations.
Be slow to anger, quick to listen, slow to speak.
In a multitude of words, sin is not lacking.
Be quick to forgive.
I speak to you about gentleness, beloved.
A gentle Word turns away wrath. I love a quiet and gentle spirit.
My son did not break even a crushed reed. There is a great healing power in gentleness...gentleness with yourself and toward others.
You fulfill all that is written when you love Me with all your heart and love others as yourself.

The enemy wants you hardened and numb.
I have given you emotions to enjoy...to laugh, love, cry, and grieve.
Don't be led by your emotions and feelings.
Be led by My Spirit. The rest is for your enjoyment.
When you look at people's faces, you can clearly see that they are wearied and burdened. I desire you to be a lifter of the burden...
a kind word is a timely encouragement.
Walk in the Spirit and you will not fulfill the desires of the flesh.
Allow Me to touch every wound, so in turn you can bring healing to others. I use you for My glory.

Day 143

My Child...

To enter My fullness, your human nature, the flesh, must be cut off.
Your divine nature is Me in you.
Your divine nature is active and frees you to hear Me.
Make no alliance with the old as you move forward
into the fullness of your inheritance.

Examine yourself and see the old ways...cut them off.
Make no provision for the flesh.
Once you become aware, bring it to the cross.
You are never alone in the process. I am with you.
My burden is easy, and My yoke is light.
Blessed are those who dwell in My house...
for they will be found singing and praising.
My love is from everlasting to everlasting for those who fear Me.
(Psalm 103:17).

Day 144

My Child...

I am the same yesterday, today, and forever. (Hebrews 13:8)
I am the Alpha and Omega...the beginning and the end...
the rock and strong tower.
I am a hiding place from the wind...a shelter from the storm.
I am like streams of water in a dry place and the shade of a great rock in a weary land. When the world and life are spiraling, and storms are all around...I am your place of refuge...
a very present help in times of trouble.
I am your strength, your lifeline, encourager, lover of your soul, guide, and helper.

You're everything to Me.
You don't fall short with Me, for with Me, you are secure
and sure-footed, beloved.
You are well-informed and able. You are able.
Bless...you are called to bless others.
Bring the light that was revealed to all mankind...
the great light that pierces all darkness, every wall and armor.
Your feet are grounded in Me.
Your feet are beautiful and carry My good news.
Your feet take ground.
Your feet move you forward, advancing steadily.
We are not two, but we are one in Jesus.

Day 145

My Child...

Understand, beloved...
I am fully committed to helping you grow and reach full maturity.
I don't see any of your faults, issues, or shortcomings.
I see the areas that need a redeemable touch from Me.

Your growth journey is a joy for Me.
I am not frustrated or disappointed with where you are at.
You can change suddenly when you allow Me to touch that area and bring change. Believe the change can come in those areas.
My arm is not too short to touch and bring change.
Come out of agreement with every issue
and anything opposing My Kingdom and My Word.
Join your spirit with My Spirit and become one with Me.
Agree with what I say about you.

Day 146

My Child...

The greatest thing I gave to you, to humanity, is love.
Be perfected in love for love casts out all fear.
Love covers a multitude of sins.
Love binds everything together in perfect harmony...
a bond of perfection.
Your love for one another shows the world you are Mine.
Follow My example, beloved.
There are things that will last forever, they are eternal.
The greatest of those is love.
See every circumstance through the lens of My Kingdom's love.

Day 147

My Child...

I never grow weary. I am long-suffering and will walk with you through every situation and circumstance.
I don't see the outward as man sees, I see the inward.
I see the motives you're longing for. I see who I created you to be.
You are one with Me in the Spirit.

Lay down every offense and every defense.
Come to Me like a child and allow others to see you as My child.
I am your protector, your defender.
I will walk with you...leading you toward the swimming experience in Me. [Ezekiel 47:2-5] I want to reveal everything to you...
step-by-step as your heart is ready. My eyes are upon you.
My eye is looking to and fro to see whose hearts are loyal to Me.
I will show myself strong on their behalf.
Arise, My beloved. Arise.

Day 148

My Child...

The hope I have poured out into your heart is an anchor for your soul. It leads you through the curtain into My inner sanctuary where the forerunner, Jesus, has entered for you...
having become your High Priest forever.
Follow in His footsteps.
You have a forerunning spirit upon you...
you have been shown the way. Walk in it.
Blaze the trail and go straight for the mark that you were shown.
I have marked each of you uniquely and purposefully.
Be single-minded, single-focused.

I am always speaking to you.
I put My Spirit in you.
I fill your mouth with Heaven's wisdom.
Eat and be filled to overflowing with the living bread.
Each day is a fresh start for you. There is no yesterday or tomorrow. Each day has enough to occupy you, so live present, in the moment and tender-hearted.
Live sensitive to My Spirit accomplishing what I have for you in the moment...abundance...the abundant life.
You as the forerunner must show others the way.
Remember, more is caught than taught...so walk in it.

Day 149

My Child...

Be careful how you walk, not as unwise but as wise...
making the best use of time because the days are evil.
Be filled with the Spirit.
Sing and make a melody to Me with your hearts.
Give thanks always and for everything.

I'm calling.
I'm calling...look to Me, leave all behind.
I'll teach your hands. I'll teach your mouth.
I'm transforming you into My image.
People will be attracted and drawn to My Spirit in you.
You have life to give them.
You have My Spirit, My words of life.
Give life to them by your words.

Day 150

My Child...

My plans and purposes will never be thwarted.
My will is in motion.
My Spirit is moving, covering, teaching, and fulfilling.
You must come in line and join in this move.
My covenant is in place and cannot be moved...it is part of the very foundations. My Word is the cornerstone of all things.

I am removing all the old. The renewing process is so important.
You are new in Me, beloved. Learn to walk in My ways.
My voice splinters the cedars of Lebanon.
My angels do My bidding.
I have set before you life and death, blessings and curses.
Therefore, choose life that you may live in My fullness.
The blood was shed for all. There is life in the blood.
A costly price was paid.

Do not tread upon the cross of Jesus by going back to former ways, the former things. Choose life. I make all things new.
Open your heart and allow Me to wash and renew, restore and repair. Raise your eyes to Me, it is where your help comes from.

Day 151

My Child...

To be close to Me is life and health for you.
More of Me, less of the world.
Put your effort towards things that last.
The worldly things will burn away like wood, hay, and straw.
Build on the foundation that has been laid
with gold, silver, and precious stones.

Be devoted to one another...
tenderly loving your fellow believers as members of one family.
Try to outdo yourselves in respect and honor of one another.
Keep a close watch on your heart,
for out of it flows the springs of life.

Day 152

My Child...

All your questions are answered while seeking Me.
I desire to reveal to you everything you need.
Quiet yourself. Be still and allow My Spirit to build your
life upon the foundation laid upon the rock of Jesus Christ.
My Spirit is building up your identity and life...
building up your family...
building up your health...
bringing you into perfection.

You are not designed for lack or emptiness.
You are My vessel...filled to overflowing...running over.
Stay connected to Me as your life-giving vine.
You will stay a beautiful, fruitful bough useful to My Kingdom.
You will see My goodness, power, and authority.
By goodness I draw and soften My children.

Jesus is your example.
Follow in his footsteps and you will receive everything.
Your emotions must stay intact, level, and enjoyable.
The high and low mood swings are not from Me.
Steady and sure-footed...
your questions are answered in My presence.

Day 153

My Child...

Your beauty is so joyful to Me, My bride, My darling.
You were grafted in...joined to Me.
Like the trunk of a tree with many branches,
I've created something in you never before seen on this earth.
You are a new creation. Do not stifle My Spirit.
It is living water within you that needs to flow down and touch the dead in people to bring life.

You are a partner of the promise in Jesus through the gospel.
Take and receive the fullness.
Do not think that when you suffer or are mistreated you are on the wrong path. Are you willing to suffer for My kingdom?
Can you endure long-suffering for My cross?
If I call you to go, will you go? Will you love?
Will you stay as a little child until the end?
Arise, and come out from behind your high, thick walls.
Let your beauty be seen by the world, My bride, My holy one.
Your voice and words will be sweet.
They will be soothing and bring peace.

Day 154

My Child...

The things of this world will compete for your time and attention.
The enemy of your life wants to wrap your mind in worry, fear, anxiety, and imaginations.
Stay aware and watch diligently for the pitfalls.
My Spirit will guide you.

I am lavishing My love upon you.
You don't have to do anything for My love.
I love you for you. I know you. I created you.
Sit in My presence and allow My Spirit to grow strong in you.
My love is unconditional.

The entrance of My Word gives light.
My Word is living and powerful, sharper than any sword.
My Word divides between soul and spirit,
discerning the thoughts and intents of the heart.
You are a carrier of My word...plant it in the hearts of men.
I will water and grow that seed.
You are a carrier of My Spirit.
You carry life...speak it forward.
Abundant life is yours, beloved.

Day 155

My Child...

I place things in your day to make you smile.
Acknowledge Me in those things...it gives Me great pleasure.
I rejoice when you rejoice. I am with you always.
Nothing in all My creation is hidden from Me.
Everything lies naked and exposed before My eyes.
I see who I created you to be.
I love you...come to Me with no pretense.
I can make the weak strong, the blind see, and the lost found.
Rejoice that I see you and love you.
Rejoice that you don't have to perform.

The fellowship and unity in My Spirit will do what is needed in you and through you. The things that you think are not coming to pass... they are not forgotten by Me.
In the fullness of time, they will happen.
Rejoice in My Kingdom and in your salvation.
Even going to the cross, there was joy set before Me.
Keep your eyes on things above.
I am the author of your faith.
I am the perfecter...the One who completes your faith.

Day 156

My Child...

I draw mankind to myself.
I have set eternity in their hearts.
How can they call on Me unless they believe?
How can they believe unless they hear?
How can they hear unless someone tells them? I touch your tongue. I make your voice sweet and melodious to the listener.

My child, I have called you according to My purpose.
My child...I draw you in. I long to draw in My family as a mother hen protects her chicks beneath her wings.
Let My Word wash you clean...
penetrating to the division of soul and spirit, joints and marrow.
My Spirit is hovering over you. My joy is washing over you.
The sweetness of the spirit and joy mingle together.

Day 157

My Child...

I am far and wide, deep and vast.
I calm you, My child. Your comfort is in Me.
He who the son sets free is free indeed.
Allow My love for you to define who you are and
how you see yourself. You are My dear one.

I am Elohim, your Mighty God. I am Lord.
I am strong and mighty, invincible in battle.
I am the King of Glory, the Lord of angel armies.
Far and wide, deep and vast...swim in the knowledge of Me.
Search My Spirit...He will reveal My deep things to you.

Ask Me for eyes to see the schemes of the enemy.
Stay far from them. There is a way that seems right in man's eyes,
but the path to Me is narrow, beloved.
Follow Me and you shall receive everything...
nothing will be held back. You will have the double-fold blessing...
the blessing of Heaven and the blessing of earth.

Day 158

My Child...

I bless those who patiently endure testing and temptation.
They will receive the crown of life that I have promised to
those who love Me. I have planted an eternity in your heart.
You are My new creation, never before seen on earth.
You have My Spirit leading you, teaching you.
Everything is available to you.
The deep things are within reach for you.
Have the kind of faith that does not doubt My Kingdom.
Stand firm.

Speak life not death. I created you to walk in the heights.
Your footing is sure and secure. I will help you.
I will uphold you with My righteous right hand as you pull
others up to My heights. Your words will be sweet in their ears.
Your counsel will change their course.
The Counselor is within you.
Trust, and do not doubt.
I will make your footing secure.
Fear not...only believe.

Day 159

My Child...

I prepare a table before you in the presence of your enemies.
My goodness and mercy shall follow you all the days of your life.
I brought you out of darkness...out from the shadow of death.
I have broken the chains that bind you.
I have broken the gates of bronze and I cut the bars of iron.
I freed you from all your distress.

I sent My Word and healed you.
I have called you with a heavenly calling.
I put My seal upon you, and I am delighted to call you My own.
I called you by name into deeper union and fellowship with Me.

Day 160

My Child...

My spirit is watching over you and the earth,
hovering and surrounding those who serve Me.
The world knows My children by their love...
their fervent zeal for Me.
Sit in My presence and hear My voice.
Go forth in boldness.
As your heart catches fire, stir and fan the flames.

I equip My saints for every good work.
Open your mouth wide and I will fill it. The kingdom is within.
Open your eyes to see and incline your ears to hear all that is around you...showers of blessing, provision, joy, peace, and righteousness. Lift your eyes to see the field ripe with harvest.
See how beautiful I have made the feet of those who go.
Hear the sweetness in voices of those who speak.
The bands are broken off your neck. Dust off the old.
Rise and shine, for My glory is dawning upon you.

Day 161

My Child...

No detail that concerns you is hidden from Me.
I see all things, I know all things.
It is not your place to question "why."
Always be joyful. Never stop praying and give thanks in all
circumstances, for this is My will for you in Christ Jesus.

There is great beauty all around.
Train yourself to see and acknowledge it.
Everything I create has a purpose, value, and beauty to be enjoyed.
Appreciate the small things. Your eye is the lamp of the body.
When your eye is healthy, your whole body is filled with light.
Keep your eyes on things above, beloved.
May the eyes of your understanding be flooded with light,
so, you may know the hope of My calling for you.

Day 162

My Child...

Come. Come, let us walk together.
There is much to learn, much to do.
This calling I have for you will not feel burdensome.
It will be a joy for you. To walk in this calling is My will for you.
You will be perfect in My great love.
I will wash and bask you in My anointing oil.

It will soften every hardened place and overcome every dry place.
I love you with a perfect love. My Spirit teaches you and brings My revelation into your core, your very depths. You will know the truth and My truth brings you freedom.
I bless you with an everlasting blessing.
There is no area, no territory left untouched or unredeemed.
Beloved, I am a God that wants 100%...
every part of you redeemed back to Me, useful to Me.
I bought it all. I redeemed it all.

My Spirit is hovering over this world. The light is dawning upon you. Reach out with both hands and grab hold of that which you have been given. My Spirit is there...always covering, teaching, and leading the way. Wash your face. Put on the oil of gladness.
Put on My love which lets the world know you are Mine.
I can make you new. I give you new thoughts, new words in your mouth, and new habits that draw us closer.

Day 163

My Child...

He who the son sets free is free indeed.
Your tongue is loose...free to teach, preach, and encourage.
Your hands are loose. They are free to be lifted in praise, lay upon the sick to be healed, and to comfort and hold the broken.
The burden on your neck, that yoke of slavery to sin, has been loosed and removed. My anointing broke the yoke and now you are free to take My yoke.

You are free, beloved.
Never go back to the things from which you were set free.
Those old things have no hold on you.
You may have a sin habit that simply needs to be replaced with the things of My Spirit, but that is simple for Me.
Set your mind on the things of My Spirit,
and you will no longer fulfill the lust of the flesh.
I desire for you to come to a place of surrender, dependent upon My Spirit...becoming one just as the three of us are one...
divine and supernatural.

Day 164

My Child...

With great joy, a mystery of your faith was revealed...
Christ in human body and justified by the Spirit.
He was seen by angels and announced to the nations.
He was believed throughout the world and taken to Heaven in glory. My desire is to reveal every mystery to you and fill you in such fullness. There is no lack.

Move forth in boldness, strength, and power.
The power for you is in the finished work of the cross.
Meditate on the cross.
Meditate on the gift that was restored to you upon the cross.
My sons and daughters have a purpose.
You are not inferior, you have been chosen. You are by design.
Your gifts were placed in you with great thought and love.
Stir them up.
Spur on one another to more than just the status quo of the world.

Day 165

My Child...

My fullness is here.
Open your ears and back out of the world's noise.
Turn toward Me. Incline your ear to hear My voice and My Word.
Speak to your ears, *"Open up."* Be sensitive to My voice.
I am always drawing you deeper. Can you hear Me? I am saying, "Walk this way," "Lay this down," "Take this up."
I am directing your steps on My path of righteousness.
The deep calls unto deep. It is never too late. You have not missed it. As long as I am giving you breath, what I have written about you can be fulfilled.

Put your hope in Me, for it will not disappoint.
I will lead you like a blind person on paths you have known, to places you have not been. I will make darkness light before you...
I will make the crooked places straight.
I am refreshing you by My Spirit, by the fullness of My Spirit.

Day 166

My Child...

If I speak, will you listen?
If I ask, will you obey?
I am searching...I am speaking. Who is hearing their shepherd?
Who will show their love through obedience to Me?
Seek and you will find Me...but seek only Me.
Call upon My name and I will say, *"Lo, I am here."*
There is a rhythm and design to My creation.
There is also time and chance. Give thanks in all things.
Seek to learn and grow in every circumstance, advancing forward and gaining ground. Guard your mind and thoughts...
let them be a garden in My Kingdom.

Knowledge is not a playground for the enemy.
Take your thoughts captive...checking them...testing them.
Where are they coming from? Be aware.
Everything found on the Rock will stand and not fall.
I have equipped you and provided weapons for warfare.
Not by the cunningness of the world but by purity of heart and innocence of a child. Have eyes to see the narrow path.
You must go in by the gate.
I call you to My side.
I invite you to enter in.
I call you, beloved.

Day 167

My Child...

Be quick to listen, slow to speak, and slow to anger, for your wrath and anger do not produce My righteousness. When you make this your practice, you won't be quick with your responses, or one who reacts. Instead, you will ponder and keep the peaceful state of your heart and mind.

Grace is available to you when your mind is free and clear of the world's clutter. There are development processes. You will think of something, plan in your heart to accomplish and achieve it, then press in and not let go, just like Jacob did when he wanted the blessing. He would not let go until he had received from Me what he set out for. [Genesis 32:22-29]
I am taking you through and this is part of your process, beloved. Allow me to have my way in this process.

Day 168

My Child...

Passion and devotion please Me.
Whatever you do, in word or deed,
do everything in the name of Jesus, giving thanks to Me.
There is a divine plan in place. A divine order to life.
When your feet are planted upon the rock of Jesus, you will not be swayed when you hear the subtle half-truths of the enemy.
You will stand firm when the storms of life come vehemently against your life. When the storm passes and the sun comes out, you will have gained peace through it all and come out on the other side with more stamina, wisdom, and strength.
You cannot fail because My kingdom is an overcoming kingdom.
My kingdom has no end.

Is something disturbing you?
It is not from Me. My kingdom bears fruit.
Even correction brings peace and joy when you understand you are being transformed into My likeness.
My perfect love casts out all fear.
The world stifles and takes from you, but in My kingdom, death gives life, surrender brings advancement, being last will put you first, and your weakness brings My strength.

Day 169

My Child...

All is well.
Let it be well with your soul.
I am a consuming fire.
Is not My word like a fire?
Is not My word like a hammer that breaks the rocks into pieces?
My Word will never pass away.
My Word will stand forever.
My Words are active and sharper than any sword piercing and dividing things that were not thought possible to separate, such as discerning thoughts and intentions of the heart.

My Word is meant to be declared, lived upon, meditated on, fixed on, abided in, and about which songs are written.
Life and health to the flesh are found by those who find my Word and keep it in their hearts. It will refresh their dryness, springing to life supernaturally...for My words are the secret and key to life.

Day 170

My Child...

You are in a fight and there needs to be a strategy.
I have given you weapons for warfare.
I teach and train your hands for war and your fingers for battle.
Your arms can bend a bow of bronze. I have given you a shield.
My right hand holds you up.
My gentleness makes you great.
Let My Word arms your tongue.
You are wearing My belt of truth.

Pull down the strongholds. Cast down imaginations and every high thing that exalts itself against My Word.
Be as cunning as a serpent and innocent as a dove.
You are My sheep in the midst of the wolves of this world.
You are My equipped saint.
You are My sent one. Go...walk...and things will be revealed.

Day 171

My Child...

I take you to the heights...
where I show you a Kingdom vantage point and view.
This will open your eyes to a new expanse and territory.
Coming into alignment with Me takes you to your next level.

Day 172

My Child...

I am the creator of all things.
I take pleasure in My creation. I look upon it all.
It is coming to completion.
I created the angelic beings to carry out My will.
I am the commander of angelic armies.
Everything under the sun has a purpose and a time.
Even your pain has a purpose, and good can come from it.

Test your heart...does it run hot and cold?
I am beckoning the world to come to Me.
I am calling My own to come near.
Will you allow Me to command you?
Will you do only what you see your father doing?

I created you with a mouth,
but it's not so you can speak whatever you want or feel.
Speak My words. I created you with free will. Freely choose Me.
I created your gifts and purpose.
You are at your best and most fulfilled
when you are walking in them and using them for My glory.

Day 173

My Child...

I give you the power to accomplish all the good things prompted by your faith. Allow My Son to be glorified through you, and you in Him according to My grace.
Jesus has been unveiled to the world.
Do you see him with unveiled eyes?
Do you understand his fullness through My word?
Search the deep things, beloved.
Each word can unveil Him more to you, My child.
Have a searching heart and I will meet you in that place.
There is never a time when your true heart's desire to know and understand goes unanswered.

Day 174

My Child...

My presence is all around.
I am represented in the cool breeze you feel on your skin.
My beauty comes forth, in every blossom on the flower.
The hope I have placed in you springs forth as the buds on a barren tree rapidly open in spring.
I have designed you to be moved by My creation...
the rolling waves lapping on the shore...
the majestic mountains that tower over you.
I love when My creation pleases you.
I love when you give Me thanks and glory.

What is catching your eye? Be aware of what gets your attention.
Observe your reaction to the situation.
What occupies your precious time on this earth?
We are on a journey together, beloved.
We are discovering together...fellowshipping together.
I touch you with a touch of awareness...
eyes open more and more.
I bring you through everything...
not by your might or by your power, but by My Spirit.

Day 175

My Child...

Where there is no vision, the people perish.
The fear of the Lord is the beginning of wisdom, knowledge of the Holy One is understanding. Let your eyes see all they need in Me.
Let your mouth speak My words back to Me and others.
Let your heart be filled to overflowing joy and fullness...
with gratefulness that you are loved with an everlasting love.
Whatever your hands find to do, do it as though you are working for Me with all that you are.
I am all things for all men.

Day 176

My Child...

Allow Me to nourish you with My Word.
Taste its sweetness as you take it in.
Allow it to penetrate deep into your core.
Allow it to remove all the impurities and purge out the old.
My Word allows truth to penetrate
and take over those areas once ruled by the enemy.
You are the victor, but the enemy wants to laugh at you
and bring to your mind every wrong move, action, and word.

You are a warrior.
The enemy wants to deceive you into giving up all your strength
and power. He is a crafty deceiver.
My Word makes scales fall off your eyes.
Deception falls away as leaves fall from a tree in the wind, with
ease and no thought. In the same way, My Word fills you with
ease...take it to your depths. Your beauty will spring forth as
daybreak pierces the night. Suddenly, your wisdom gained from
the Word will shine as diamonds. It will be sought after.

I am Elohim, your Mighty God.
I want to show myself strong on your behalf.
I draw your heart closer to My heart.
I want all that you are.
I leave nothing untouched by My love and grace.

Day 177

My Child...

You have been saved...snatched out of the fire and gloriously redeemed to be a redemptive fire for people.
Your hope and your future should fill you with blissful joy.
The momentary pain and problems do not compare with the good I have for you all around. I am your great reward.
My heart is tender toward you, My beloved one.
I am the God of "more than enough."
I cover you with My glory...giving you a garment of praise.
I am the God of all eternity.
Change your mindset from temporal to eternal and it will take you to a new level of seeing and understanding.

Day 178

My Child...

Why do you call to Me, *"Lord, Lord,"* yet you do not do what I say?
Allow My Spirit to move and motivate all that you do.
Unity in My Spirit is powerful.
Come together often in prayer and agreement.
Do not be alarmed when you see the world acting worldly.
I have written this time in My Word.
Stand on My Word...My written will for you.
I am Elohim, your Mighty God. Mighty in battle.

As a man thinks in his heart, so he is.
Align your mind, your heart, and your thoughts with My Word.
The old man is cast off...cut off. He has been crucified and buried.
Walk in the new. Why look back to the old man...those old ways...those old wineskins. No one puts new wine in old wineskins, for it will burst, and the new wine is lost.

The new wine of My revelation belongs in new wineskins.
You are a new creation never before seen on this earth.
There are those who have longed to see and are now seeing My Sons and daughters who are the dwelling place for My Spirit.
You are the temples.
They look unto you with awe and wonder...with splendor.
There is a great cloud of witnesses watching you,
praying for you and rejoicing with great joy over you.

Day 179

My Child...

Put away the things of this world.
Come out from among those in the world and separate yourselves.
Purify your mouth, your heart, and your thoughts.
You are useful to your Master.
Above all, let love be your motivation.
Surrender yourself into My hands.
You are the clay, and I am the potter.
I will form and fashion you into the vessel I need.

My kingdom is like a hidden treasure that you discover then sell everything to purchase it. My Kingdom requires all from you.
In turn, you get all from Me.
My Kingdom must take all that you are,
so you can receive all that I am.
Do not fear the process of dying to yourself.
Allow joy to flow over you while this is happening over your life.
This is a constant process bringing you into perfection...completion in Me. Your process of refinement is precious to Me.
I take great joy in it.

Day 180

My Child...

You are all running your race on this earth.
Do not look to the right or to the left.
Allow each person their process.
Why is someone else's race making you stumble?
Put your hand to the plow. Don't look back.
Keep occupied with your task at hand...not with anyone else...not on tomorrow...for in this day is enough to keep you fully occupied.

Thank Me for today's provision and don't wonder about tomorrow.
For I am your Father, and I know what you need.
Your worry is a 'lack' mentality.
It is not of your Father in Heaven.
For I own the cattle on a thousand hills. Everything is Mine.
Your worry is a lack of trust in Me. Release...let go.

One must be willing to die to self to produce much fruit.
If a grain of wheat falls to the ground and dies,
it produces exponentially.
A soldier does not get entangled in civilian affairs...
he does what pleases his commanding officer.
If he is entangled, he cannot carry out his orders.

My peace I give you, not as the world gives do I give.
You are not what the world says you are.
You are My creation, and you are what I say about you.
I have given you your identity...
so shed what the world has said and put on what I have said.

Day 181

My Child...

You are the carriers of My Spirit. You carry My kingdom.
Your level of surrender determines how much I can work through you and how much of My kingdom you carry.
You can change the atmosphere anywhere you go.
You can change cultures, you can be a role model in this generation. If you throw a tiny pebble in a pond,
it will create a small splash and a few ripples.
If you throw a stone, a larger, splash and more ripples are created.
If you throw a boulder, you get a tremendous reaction.
You are the stone in My hand,
and I am using you in the way I have perfectly designed.

You are up above, not below.
Incline your ear to Me, for I am speaking.
I am calling your mind to pay attention to My Kingdom.
I am developing you into a being of My likeness.
I want to see every attribute of My Son in you.
If your eyes are on Me, you can see everything counterfeit and you will not stray...but stay close to your Shepherd.

Day 182

My Child...

My kingdom is by design.
There is timing and precision.
Search My Word and the Holy Spirit will lead you into its deep meanings and mysteries.
There is purpose and meaning in every word and story.
Enjoy your time here, your time is short.
Savor the moments, the fullness, and the joy.
When it is in your power to do good, do it.
Don't let the moment pass by, for it may not come again.

Join yourself to Me, attach and hold fast.
We must be knit together supernaturally. We are bound.
Whatever you find yourself doing, do it with all your heart and effort, as though you were doing it for Me.
I will be right there with you. I will see your heart and efforts and reward you accordingly.
Be willing, and think in your mind, "God is able, and He will give me the grace to accomplish and achieve."
You must be willing to come down in order to go to higher ground.

Day 183

My Child...

You worry about many things, but only one thing is necessary.
There are substitutions all around.
My Spirit will lead you to the truth.
Study My Word to learn My character, My love, and My plan.
Gain understanding and seek after wisdom.

Do not be one who worships Me with your mouth,
but your heart is far from Me.
Knit your heart to My heart.
I want all that you are...hold nothing back from Me.
Be a builder of man, not one who tears down.
Build your life upon My foundation,
and teach others how to do the same.

I have washed you clean. You are white as snow.
I have given you a robe of righteousness.
I have clothed you in My goodness and My mercy follows you every day of your life. My mercies meet you every morning as you wake up to new revelations in Me. Time keeps rolling on.

Generations come and go, but only one thing will remain forever, beloved. Hunger and thirst after it...hunger and thirst after it.
Be one who contemplates...who ponders My deep truths.
Those who fall away leave a hole, a bare spot in the flock.
Call the backslidden to return. Open your mouth wide in intercession and command them back.
Let love be what you are known for.

Day 184

My Child...

I am all things for all mankind.
I am growing all things through Me.
You have been created as one body with many parts,
working together in unity for a common need and goal.
Be devoted to one another in brotherly love.
Be diligent and passionate for the things of My Spirit.
Shouldn't life in My Spirit be zealous? Shouldn't life in My Spirit be overcoming since I overcame this world?

I made you alive together with Me. I took everything that has ever been or could ever be used against you and nailed it to the cross.
I canceled every debt you owed. I paid it in full.
I disarmed every ruler and all the authorities.
I put them on public display, having triumphed over them.
Therefore, you can have boldness in the finished work of the cross.
I finished My race and sit at the right hand of My Father.
Now you are running your race to completion.
Do it with excellence and confidence,
knowing that you are here by My design.

You are one with plans and purposes.
You are your Father's child.
You look like Me.
You act like Me.
You sound like Me.
You are My beloved child with My DNA grafted in.

You are My very own special treasure, never before seen on this earth. Not confused in what you are doing, but you set yourself like flint on your path of destiny to do all things...
everything for which I have ordained and set you apart.
It is not over...it is not too late...it is not derailed.
It will happen...just believe.

Day 185

My Child...

I spoke My Word of power as creation came into being.
I spoke My creative power into your very being, cascading
revelation light into every part of your very fabric.
When you cease striving and enter the Sabbath,
you will rest in completion and maturity.
In the beginning, as soon as I created you,
you came into rest with Me.
Stay in that posture of rest as you take dominion over your
territory and subdue it. You are designed to rule and reign.
There is such a beautiful design and creative order to My creation,
so fear not...go forth in peace and boldness.

My righteous ones live by faith.
You were not designed for measure. You are not limited.
The heights and depths and widths are yours to explore.
Your boundaries have fallen in pleasant places.
Fix your eyes on Me.
Plant your feet upon My rock.
Steady and stay your heart upon My heart.
Feel My great love for you...cascading over you and your situations.
Feel My great love creating new avenues to walk upon...
illuminating new thoughts that create new paths.
Creation is always happening. I am a creator, it is My nature.

Day 186

My Child...

Allow Me to inspire you.
Let My inspiration rise...giving you dreams and visions.
There is a great harvest within you.
There are beautiful things I have planted within you that are still in the process of growing and blooming. Your true act of worship is offering your life as a living sacrifice to Me.
Allow My Spirit to bring forth everything in you.

Showers of blessings are around your life like the dew of Hermon that comes down upon the mountain of Zion. I command My blessing...life forevermore.
I want you to know there is so much more.
There is more to delight in...wonder, awe, and joy.
Explore the depths, beloved child.
Ask Me for what your heart desires.
Journey through this life with Me in oneness of heart,
oneness of Spirit, and oneness of way. We are the same.
You live and move and have your being in Me.
This journey we are on is simple.
Life in the Spirit is simple, pure, and lovely.
The enemy would have you think it is burdensome,
but My yoke is easy, My child.

Day 187

My Child...

Live your precious life as a living reflection of Me. Every attribute I have should be reflected in your words, deeds, and actions.
When the enemy looks to find grounds of accusation or evidence of corruption, let none be found because you are trustworthy and there is no negligence or corruption found in you.
Live in the understanding that I see all things,
whether in the open or in secret.
I know your heart is to please Me.

Renewal is taking place. A shedding off and putting on
is a constant cycle in the lives of My children.
Renewal...renewal is a must.
The world can apply such pressure.
You have a kingdom living inside of you.

The kingdom has greater pressure and persuasion for good that surpasses anything the enemy can apply. I always make a way.
You will not be tempted beyond what you are able to endure. You will grow up into all things in Me through each of these processes.

Day 188

My Child...

There is so much knowledge I want you to gain, but you will not receive it through worldly wisdom. That is of no use to you...
for worldly knowledge leads to trusting in your own understanding.
My knowledge brings understanding. Understanding brings wisdom.
When you read My word, it will be a delight to you...
knowing that understanding follows. This will increase the grace in your life to live in this fallen world and not be troubled when you see difficulties of every kind.

For in this time, people are lovers of self and lovers of money... proud, arrogant, abusive, disobedient to their parents, ungrateful, unholy, heartless, without self-control, lovers of pleasure rather than lovers of Me. Some will even have the appearance of godliness but deny My power. Avoid such people beloved.

My Word is a lamp to your feet and a light to your path.
My Word highlights the traps and pitfalls.
This life is short. Those traps and wrong paths can devour years upon years, so stay close to Me.
Do not fear...I can redeem the time the enemy has stolen.
Give no more time to him.
Beloved, if you could grasp how full your life in the Spirit with Me will be, you would laugh and skip and jump and leap while waiting with great anticipation to see what I will do next for you.

Your Father who loves you is here smiling over you.
I take great delight in you...
I have thoughts and dreams about you as numerous
as the grains of sand on every seashore.
I am prophesying good works, plans, and purposes for you.
Don't worry. Don't fear.
Just rejoice. Again, I say have the rejoicing experience.

Day 189

My Child My Child...

I am free-flowing and expansive.
I cannot be contained in your mind,
which has limited knowledge and understanding.
Putting Me into your parameters and abilities will keep you in a small place. Be at peace with not understanding everything.
Be at peace with My mystery.
I know you want to know and understand Me.
Focus on having a relationship with Me.
Dedicate yourself to prayer, rest, My word, and abiding in Me.
Things will be revealed and become clear to you.
Greater knowledge and understanding will occur naturally.

Be teachable, for My Spirit is with you always...
waiting to pour into you at all times...waiting to show you your path, gifts, talents, and all the things you need.
Be moldable...even in areas where you feel victorious.
Realize those are your parameters of victory, not Mine.
There are levels upon levels of victory, beloved. Isn't that exciting?
Isn't it nearly impossible to work with hardened, dry clay?
Hardness where you are concerned is of the enemy.
Simply add the oil of gladness to your life.
Gladness and a thankful heart will create that supple softness needed to stay moldable.
When you walk in meekness and gentleness, My power and authority blossom.

Day 190

My Child...

With a heart that is right before Me,
I can do all things for you and through you.
Tenderly care for My sheep, My beloved child,
and be tender with your own heart.
I work with each one of you uniquely,
just as I have designed you as one of a kind.
You are My special treasure,
used for a specific purpose on this earth for My Kingdom.

Looking to others is a pitfall.
You have something they don't have.
This life is a gift and has great purpose.
I understand it can get tedious and worrisome but learn to
encourage yourself in Me. Allow My Spirit to minister to you.
Take time to laugh and be light in My presence. Nothing is wasted.
Everything has purpose. This may be outside of your
understanding, so, you need to trust Me.

I meet you where you are at on your journey.
There is no condemnation in Me.
I love your process and your journey.
I take great joy in watching you develop and grow in Me.
As you are becoming, you are reaching for others to become.
You are uncovering and discovering that which I have placed inside
of you...that divine nature.

Day 191

My Child...

Watch over your words.
I have set before you life and death, blessings and curses.
Choose life that you may live, and it will be well with your soul.
He who has ears to hear and puts this into practice,
keeps himself far from trouble.
You are a creator...create life with your words.
Build others up by the love and grace that pours forth by your spirit. Help others dream big and see its fulfillment through your encouragement and prayer.
Rejoice and do good. Be known as one who glorifies your Father, one who carries goodness and mercy wherever you go.
Let My joy and gladness be seen upon your face.

Rejoice, again I say rejoice.
Recall the many blessings I have rained down upon you.
My faithfulness will walk you through every trial and tribulation.
Your Father in heaven knows everything you need.
I see what you are walking through and what is coming next.
Give thanks for all things and in every situation because I am with you in all things and through all things.
Your joy is complete in Me.
Your issues have solutions through Me.
Cast all your cares upon Me for I care for you. No good thing do I withhold from the one who walks uprightly before Me.

Day 192

My Child...

Surrender.
You think and feel good with the status quo...
a man's ways seem good in his own eyes.
It takes your surrender even in the areas where you feel good.
Those are the very areas I desire to stir up for your good.
Allow Me to elevate those areas.
Go to the emptying place, beloved.
I cannot occupy that which is already full.
The starting point is in your mind with the revelation that change is needed. More is required to go to the depths...a place of surrender. Come to Me and pour out your heart...your burdens, worries, and troubles. Tell it all to Me. Hold fast unto Me.

Determine in your heart and mind that you won't let go until you have victory in those areas. Nothing should overtake you, beloved. For you were designed to rule and reign...
to subdue and take ground.
Don't be satisfied with what has been.

Surrender.
Desire fullness and victory in those areas.
You feel, know, and understand those constraints...
those limitations that should not be. You have been crucified.
It is no longer you who live, beloved. Ponder that.

It is no longer you who is living, but Christ Jesus,
My Son, who lives in you. He came to give you all that He is.
This life you are now living is lived by faith in Him.
He gave you all so you could be all.
No shortages...no limitations. All that He is lives in you.
Meditate on that truth then surrender to it. This is a key, beloved.

Don't accept what has been in the past, for it is so far below what is available to you now. Say no to your flesh.
Be strong and stand your ground so that fleshly part will be crucified and come under the authority of My Spirit.

Day 193

My Child...

I can minister all things to your heart and spirit.
Look to Me to provide all things naturally and spiritually.
I can fill what you are lacking for there is no lack in My Kingdom.
Pull down every expectation you have,
and take up surrender and trust in Me for your life.
I hold everything in the palm of My hand.

I have fashioned you in your mother's womb.
I renew your mind with My Word.
Come into agreement with Me, beloved.
Let your heart say, *"Yes, and Amen," "Yes, and Amen."*
Let your heart rejoice in saying *"Let it be for me."*

What is a stumbling block for you?
Tell Me all about it and together we will break through.
See yourself as a victor...
a victorious one who succeeds in word and deed.
The next level is here, step into more.
I am beckoning you.

Day 194

My Child...

Allow My plans and purposes to have their way in your life.
Allow My timing to come about. Prepare your life before Me.
I receive all you do as an offering.
Your prayers come up before Me...filling the bowls of heaven.
Your prayers come up before Me as a fragrant and pleasing aroma.
Your acts of service and kindness are seen and written in My book.

It is written in the book of remembrance when you remember Me
and My Kingdom, and when you step out in obedience and faith.
You are seen and you are heard.
What you do in secret, I will reward openly.
Your suffering for My kingdom will be rewarded.

Everything has a purpose.
Nothing is too far gone for Me to renew and rekindle.
Believe in Me for what seems impossible to you.
Set yourself apart from worldly things and things that draw you
into traps. Come out and be separate.
Do you not know that a little leaven works through the whole
lump? Do not fear loneliness...I am with you filling every lack.

I will fill you with wisdom.
There is always a way. There is always a solution.
Seek My wisdom more than you seek the world.
Allow My zeal to come upon you and burn
away all the chaff and distractions.
Come My Child, speak to Me.
Let's talk and reason.
Let's have such a special relationship.
You are Mine and I am yours.

Day 195

My Child...

The law was given so you know what is of Me and not from Me.
My Spirit was put into you to lead you into all truth.
Diligently put My Word into your heart.
It is living and active. It is a divider and a discerner in your life.
Live in My truth, for My truth is absolute. Only by knowing My truth can you see the areas of your flesh where the enemy operates. Give no room to the enemy.

Set yourself apart and be holy for Me...
living your life poured out as a living sacrifice.
In word and deed, do all for Me.
Sit in My presence...soak in My glory.
I will make you fishers of Men.
People will be drawn to My Spirit in you. They will hear your voice as comfort and receive you as a delight...like a fresh wind blowing and awakening their spirit to respond to Me through you.

Most of My children are so entangled by their own lives they are rendered ineffective to My Kingdom.
You are here by My design and for My purpose.
I cut away the bands that held you.
Don't return to that entrapment.
Run your race...seek Me and run your race.
Seek Me...put your hand to the plow and don't look back.
When you seek Me with all your heart, you will find Me.
You have a cloud of heavenly witnesses cheering for you, praying for your victory. You are one with a great calling and purpose.
Enter wholeheartedly with Me, enter in.

Day 196

(From the author: He showed Me a glimpse of His joy as He formed you in your mother's womb.)

My Child...

I delighted in giving you your gifts and personality.
I took your book and wrote out your destiny. My plans and purposes for you were written in detail, with great care.
I have hope and faith that you will accomplish all I have planned for you. It is vital you understand your value, purpose, and design.
The enemy attacks your identity because it is your starting place, your true north, your rock, and your sure foundation.

Without your identity rooted and grounded in the truth of Me, you will be like a wave tossed to and fro in the ocean. You will believe lies, wound yourself, and come into agreement with lies that are powerful. I designed agreement, but agreement is to be only with My Word.

The enemy fears you, so he attacks.
Fear not...for I am with you.
He cannot remove what I have said about you.
Neither can your gifts be taken nor your deep ability to forgive, love, and repent...turning your heart back to My heart.
You can choose...for I created you with free will.

Day 197

My Child...

If you are looking to the world,
it will let you down and lead you into discouragement.
If the world granted you acceptance, that would not be of Me.
The world rejected Me so it will reject you.
What is your need? I am longing to fill it.
I want to see your face shining in the reflection of My face.
I want to see My joy beaming out from your smile.
I make all things beautiful in My time.

Walk in holiness before Me.
I comfort you with an everlasting comfort.
I receive you, receive all from Me.
Take My hand and seek My face early in the morning.
I put My wounded hand upon your head to take all your wounding in My body.

Day 198

My Child...

I make all things beautiful in My timing. I created all things in heaven and on the earth...the visible and the invisible.
What created thing can thwart My plans?
There is no need to strive.
Let no one add to My word, loading you down with burdens.
Simply have faith in My word.
Love Me and love others.
When you see something, pray.
Bring it to Me...then be assured that I have heard you, and the word that you spoke, together with your faith, will cause it to happen.

Let go of timing and hold fast to the thought, *"It is in process."*
Expect it to happen and thank Me that I heard and that I am working in that area. Have confidence in what I am doing more than you have confidence in what you are seeing in the natural.
Have faith in the invisible that is at work,
and you will receive what you have prayed for.
Your creator has heard your cry.
Come into agreement with Me.

Day 199

My Child...

I am the wisdom from above. When you lack wisdom in any area, ask Me and I will give to you generously without shame or reproach. When you allow My Word to dwell in you richly, wisdom flows easily. Look and see where your mind wanders in quiet times. Listen and hear what is coming through your mouth out of the abundance of your heart.
This will show you what is richly dwelling in you.

There is no condemnation in Me. I bring correction to those I love, My beloved children...in whom I delight.
Direct your mind to meditate on My living Word.
The entrance of My Word brings light.
My wisdom from above is pure...peaceful, gentle, open to reason, full of mercy and good fruit, impartial and sincere.
My wisdom is better than jewels. It brings understanding.
It is a blessing to those who find it.

Listen to advice and accept instruction, that you may gain wisdom.
Seek it more than financial wealth and gain.
What are you asking Me for daily?
Is wisdom among your requests?
This is life and health to you.
Ask and keep on asking...
then you will have the life-giving gift of My wisdom from above.

Day 200

My Child ...

There is blindness from the enemy and there is a divine blindness. (Isaiah 42:19) A choice to be blind to the things of this world. Pray the enemy's blinders come off fully...
for you know in part and you prophesy in part.
Saul was boldly and blindly carrying out his desires and will, but when he encountered My son, the blinders fell off and he became My witness of mercy and honor.
He became My servant who is blind and My messenger who is deaf. Blind to this world and all its pulls. Deaf to gossip and offense.
Push forward to take hold of that which you were taken hold of for...the kingdom of God. Search your heart.

When you seek, ask, and knock you will find Me, and I will hear you. Understand that you have blinders and limitations...
then open your mouth wide so that I may fill it.
I fill you to overflowing with My good Spirit.
Intercede for one another, for all the saints.
Open your mouth in praise and rejoicing.
Sing songs to Me out of the overflow of your heart.
Arise, My beloved one. Arise and shine...
for the light of this world has dawned upon you.
This is your devotion. This is the good and praiseworthy reality to live in and feed on daily. You must lose your life to gain life in Me. Have no fear, for what will I not do for the one who walks upright before Me? None can overtake you, beloved.

Day 201

My Child...

I created you to do good.
I am good...goodness is one of the aspects of My nature.
I am delighted to do good for you.
I designed goodness to go before you,
to be upon you and all around you...to follow after you.
Be attached to Me. Connect with My body, mind, soul, and Spirit.
When you are unburdened and free, praise and thanksgiving flow easily from your mouth. When you are burdened, there is a tightness and heaviness where praise is concerned.

Be alert and aware...
the enemy waits and watches for an opportune time to come in.
I have declared that you are a watchman on the wall.
I gave you your life, now lend it back to Me every day.
See yourselves as My peacemakers, as My comforters,
My encouraging uplifters. Love My sheep and take care of My flock...praying for the saints. You are My champion.
Step out of your comfort zone and ask for what you want.
You have not, because you ask not.

Day 202

My Child...

Have no fear.
I am like a loving mother, wanting to gather you in My arms...
rocking and comforting you when you need it.
I am your strong tower.
Run to Me and be strengthened in your inner man.
Then you will run and not grow faint or weary.
I train you to stand and fight with My weapons of warfare that are for pulling down strongholds-of the enemy.
When others see you stand, you will show them how they can stand in My strength and My strong tower.

Live your life as a testimony to Me. Let your light shine before men so that they see your good works and glorify Me.
Most people are crumbling under the yoke of the enemy,
but you are walking easily through the valley of the shadow of death, for I am with you. My rod and staff, they comfort you.
I am pointing the way and protecting you...
be confident in Me and place yourself so lovingly into My hands.
I gave you life and you handed your life back to Me.
I rejoice in this, beloved. I hold you secure in My palm.
I have engraved you on the palm of My hand.
Choose Me daily.
Choose Me in the word.
Choose Me in deed.
In all you do, reflect Me.

Day 203

My Child...

Seek My face, for I desire to be your constant companion.
The world has so much to draw you in, but it's a façade and has nothing to offer you except heartache, pain, and confusion.
Come close to Me and I will come close to you.
Wash your hands and purify your heart.
Let not your heart and loyalty be divided between Me and the world anymore. On this earth, My children go through many things.

Encounter Me.
One touch is all that is needed, like My daughter with the issue of blood who thought, *"If I could just touch Jesus, I will be healed."*
She determined to encounter Him that day.
The crowds of people also had needs,
but their hearts were divided in loyalty.
She determined to draw close, and I became her heart's focus.
I became her desire and greatest need, the One she hoped in and sought after. She fought to get to Me.
She set her heart upon Me and found what she was seeking.
Her close champion. Her champion, creator, and restorer.
Seek My face, beloved.

Day 204

My Child...

I am doing a new thing. Can you not perceive it?
A new thing requires a new man, a new lens through which to see.
Attach to Me in mind, body, soul, and spirit.
When you move toward Me in attachment,
a detachment from the world is the natural counterpart.
No matter the circumstance or situation, don't let your heart be troubled, for the I Am is with you.
I am bringing you into a new thing.
Growth can cause discomfort and pain, but it produces a treasure.
Be joyful during life's processes...
allow your countenance to reflect My goodness and joy so that others might see you and be drawn to Me through you.

One aspect of My nature is that of a nurturer.
I long to draw you in and hold you...
providing for you and sheltering you tenderly.
In My all-sufficient presence, even the darkness becomes light.
You can walk easily through the shadow of darkness
because My light is upon your head. Not natural, but supernatural.
Beloved, the natural mind cannot comprehend Kingdom thinking.
Let your mind be renewed by My Kingdom and My truth.

Day 205

My Child...

Encounter Me for a new mindset...
a new viewpoint and vantage point.
Many have heard of Me, but now I want your eyes to see Me...
experience oneness and intimacy with Me.

Come soar with Me above the natural realm
into the supernatural realm...live in that place.
I have placed every gift inside of you.
Everything you need to fulfill your destiny and calling is within.
Fan the flames and ignite the things within. Live as My flames of fire with divine zeal and passion for My Kingdom.
Many are called, but few respond.

Day 206

My Child...

Jesus must be the cornerstone of your life, the chief foundation on which your life is constructed...for any other foundation is shifting sand. Have you ever planted your feet in the sand, on the shoreline, allowing the waves to flow over and over again? Notice how your feet sink further and further down as the sand covers and settles over them...layer upon layer.
You almost fall over pulling them out.

This is a picture of foundations.
If your life is wearing you out, check where your feet are planted. Be equipped. Come into the unity of faith and of the knowledge of My Son, a perfect man. Then you will no longer be tossed to and fro, carried about with every wind of doctrine,
or by the trickery of men.

How tiring is it when you are unstable in all your ways?
I have set your feet upon the rock, and I have placed your boundaries in pleasant places.
It is you who is stepping off the rock into the sand, beloved.
But no one can snatch you from Me.
It's only in your power that can happen.

I will not let you be tempted beyond what you are able. When temptation comes, I will provide the way of escape, so you are able to endure it. Flee from the love of the things of this world.

Day 207

My Child...

Look to Me to refresh you daily.
The strife with others can take its toll on you.
Remember your forefathers this day.
They sacrificed upon altars to Me.
In the New Testament, you are the altar of earth...
make your life a living sacrifice to Me daily.
Sacrifice your time, your finances, your will... your very life.
Your forefathers lived in temporary tents as they sojourned.
You are an ambassador on this earth for a brief time to accomplish My plan and purpose for your life by My Kingdom design.

Wells were vital for your forefathers.
They built their lives around them.
I am your well of salvation. (Isaiah 12:3)
I dwell in you, My child.
I am the well of the Living One who watches over you.
It's not the season of visitation but of habitation.
It is a well of perpetual revelation and grace.
It is the place where I see your problems and provide a well of mercy and satisfaction. It is not a physical place you live close to...
it is a welling up within you as your source of supply.

Day 208

My Child...

I have ordained this day.
I have a plan, a divine order and timing.
Nothing escapes My eyes. Nothing is hidden from Me.
All things lay bare before Me, there is no creature hidden from Me.

There will be a day when all will give an account before Me.
Fear and great reverence before Me are the beginning of wisdom.
Knowledge of My Son will bring you great understanding.
Apply with understanding the wisdom I have poured out.
My wisdom should be sought after.
It is to be cherished more than wealth.

Be slow to speak and slow to anger,
for the anger of man does not produce My righteousness.
Be quick to listen and receive that which is good, solid, right, pure, and lovely. Speak goodness...share from your heart the nuggets I have given you. Be passionate where My Kingdom is concerned.
My ways are gentle and persistent.

I am passionate in the pursuit of My children like the gentle rolling waves that come onto the shore, one after another.
I am there pursuing each of you with My great love.
I continue to call you up to greater levels.
You can hear Me beckoning and leading you...
giving you glimpses of where I want you to go...
what I want you to do.

I mark My own.
I sealed them in My love,
and they cannot be snatched from My hand.
You can see and hear them.
You are drawn to them.
My own know My voice.
They follow Me...they look like Me and sound like Me.
They are My special treasure.
Carry My grace and glory, My child.

Day 209

My Child...

Remain in Me. Abide in Me and I in you.
I want you to have a deeper revelation of how we are to walk together, for you live, move, and have your being in Me.
Think of how I designed babies to be attached to their mothers in the womb by the umbilical cord. It supplies all the baby's needs.
This is a picture of our attachment.
It is a constant flow of everything you need.
We are to be as one...dwelling together as one.
Adjust your mindset...we are not two but one.
You are in Me, and I in you.

It is a supernatural event that happened when you received Me by faith. We came to dwell within you.
It is a deep and abiding attachment,
a direct connection to My Kingdom...the Heavenly realm.
It is a place where nothing is impossible.
The place where the miraculous happens.
I have no boundaries or geographical borders.
You are free in Me to do everything.
You are unhindered in all your ways.
The baby's whole world is right there in that place of attachment.
There is no stress or strain.
The process simply happens through attachment.
Beloved, your process will happen through your attachment to Me.

Day 210

My Child ...

I am your God...I am near.
I see your pain and I hear your cry.
I have great mercy and compassion for the downcast and rejected.
It is My very nature to be drawn to the hurting, broken,
poor, and rejected. I love to bring honor to the dishonored ones.
This natural realm and your circumstances do not reflect your
value, worth, or the identity I have assigned to you. It is of utmost
importance that you know how greatly you are loved.

Open your heart to Me. Turn your eyes upon Me, and a new level
of grace will be opened to you...touching every one of those places.
Turn your eyes upon Me and you will become a true worshiper of
Me...the Almighty One. Find your fulfillment in Me.
Your circumstances will either break you and take you from Me or
your circumstances will propel you to attach and depend upon Me.

The pillars of the earth are Mine.
I have set the world upon them.
I am the defender of the poor and needy.
My heart is touched by your cry.
I have chosen the poor of this world to be rich in faith.
I am your great reward. I will save you out of all your troubles,
and set your feet upon a steady place, the Rock.

Day 211

My Child...

Creativity comes from Me.
I want to give you creative ways to do things, and the ability to transcend traditional ideas, rules, patterns, and relationships.
I want to give you ways to create meaningful new ideas, forms, methods, and interpretations with the heart and simplicity of a child. I want to give you great dreams.
I want to penetrate every area of your life, spirit, soul, mind, and body with My Kingdom realm.

I want to show you what no eye has seen, and no ear has heard...
the deep mysteries I have chosen for you,
for such a time as this, beloved.
The time is now. I am a God of fullness.
Fullness now...during your process.
You don't receive it at the finish line...
it is something to be walked in now.

Day 212

My Child...

Look at your life...
What fruit being produced in your life?
What emotions are you experiencing?
The fruit of one walking with Me is love, joy, peace, patience, kindness, goodness, faithfulness, gentleness, and self-control.
Are you overwhelmed, tired, frustrated?
Check your life and see what is causing this fruit.
I do not want you to be blind...groping in the dark...
doing things out of habit that you learned from the world.
The things of this world must feel foreign to you.
I must occupy your heart, mind, and speech so I can fill you with laughter, praise, and joy...overflowing from you like a living stream.

Beloved, all things are permissible,
but not all things are constructive for you.
At times, My followers were beaten, imprisoned,
and still singing praises to Me with joy in their hearts.
Detach from worldly bonds and mindsets.
What you encounter during this life cannot compare to what is in store for you. This is not your home...you are passing through on your journey home. I have set eternity in your heart.
You feel that and you know that.
You are My representative here...
My hands and My feet...My mouthpiece.
I have sent you, so go. You can comfort the hurting.
You can edify the hearer.

Day 213

My Child...

Deposits into you have been made.
Deposit My Word into your entire being.
Saturate yourself until nothing remains of the old man.
Seek to do good. You grieve the Holy Spirit when you hurt people with your actions. Let My grace-filled love flood into every part of your being. You will not fall short in any area.

I have called you and I have provided the grace for every good work. Treat everyone in the same manner you want to be treated. I place a high value on each of you. Do the same...see the value of My children and act with gentleness and kindness.
The tongue of the wise brings healing and edification.
I clothed you in righteousness.
I covered you with a garment of praise.
Offer a sacrifice of praise in every situation.

Free your mind and emotions so that I can pour out dreams, visions, and directions for the next steps I want you to take.
There is beauty in the moments of life.
Rejoice in the anticipation of the next steps
and in every part of your process.
This is the day that I have made.
Rejoice and be glad in it.

Day 214

My Child...

I am speaking to My beloved children.
Do you have ears to hear Me?
I am showing you the way to walk.
Do you have eyes to see Me on the path?
Do not let your heart be troubled.
Return to your first love.
Enjoy those you love. Be quick to listen and quick to forgive.
Love covers a multitude of sins.
A quiet and gentle spirit is precious in My sight.
Let all you do be motivated from a place of love.
I see each motive behind every action.
All things are known to Me. They lay bare right in front of Me,
so be innocent like a small child.
Be wide-eyed with wonder for My great love for you.
Let that love be your motivator to believe all things.

Allow My love to give you the grace to endure all things.
The greatest of all things is love.
I am the Lord, the God of all the flesh
and I poured out My Spirit upon you.

Day 215

My Child...

Commune with Me. Communing with Me will bring your spirit back into alignment with Me. From My dwelling place,
I look upon all My children on the earth...
I fashioned your hearts individually.
I see all your works.
I see the works prompted by your faith.
Great is My faithfulness to you, beloved.
There may be times when the old nature rises, but you are a new creation, and those old ways and patterns of life will feel foreign. You will put them off with ease and step back onto the path of life ordered by Me.

You have been marked. You bear the mark of My Beloved Son. That is your identity...the true you.
I have given you such divine and extravagant gifts...
I have given you the most beautiful nature, one that has no breaking point or boiling point.
My nature is every fruit of the Spirit which has been grafted into you. You have My DNA, you bear My mark upon you.
I have marked you as a builder.
Build My Kingdom with kindness that flows from you and pours into people's lives. Build My Kingdom.
Build with your actions, words, and deeds.

Day 216

My Child...

I want you to be wise and aware of the schemes and traps of the enemy. I desire that you walk in fellowship with other believers so that you may sharpen and strengthen one another, spurring each other on to the good works that I have prepared for you.

A trap of the enemy is to cut you off and isolate you.
Be aware of those wanting you to come away.
You are designed for fellowship and unity.
Do not forsake the gathering together of the assembly.
You see the birds flying in their V formation. They use one another to fly longer, faster, and with less energy and force. Just as dolphins can be found riding the wake of a boat, they frolic and enjoy the pull. They understand it helps them go further and faster with less output of energy.

So, walk together, rejoicing and sharing each other's joys and burdens. When you spend time in My presence, you are being molded and changed into My image and likeness.
Just as My glory was reflected on Moses' face, My likeness is upon you where others will see it and be changed by it.
There must be an aligning that happens between us.
Align your soul and your body with My Spirit.

Meet the Author

Jennifer Turner is an ordained pastor, teacher, mother of two grown children, and wife of Evangelist David Turner. For the past 20 years, she has traveled the world with her husband ministering the gospel of Jesus Christ. She saw countless miracles and healings that stirred in her a desire for a deeper, more intimate relationship with the living God.

Jennifer earnestly desired the gift of tongues. She was intrigued and fascinated when different languages began to flow from within, and delighted when she could recognize different dialects.

Upon reading Paul's encouragement in 1 Corinthians 14:13, *"The one who speaks in tongues is to pray for the interpretation,"* Jennifer began to sit with an open journal ready to hear the interpretations. For over a year, she waited joyfully and expectantly. As the Holy Spirit began to put the words in her heart, the floodgates were opened and the gift developed beautifully. This book is the fruit of that process.

Just as the Bible says, *"Elijah was an ordinary man like you and I,"* (James 5:17) Jennifer is an ordinary woman with an extraordinary, supernatural relationship with the Lord Jesus Christ.

Epilogue

Beloved children of the Most High God,

My love and greetings to the readers of this book, **My Child... *God Speaks to His Children*.** This book is the direct revelation of the Holy Spirit given to my daughter, Jennifer Turner, during meditation and prayer.

Beloved readers, God has chosen you in heavenly places, in Christ Jesus, by giving all spiritual blessings before you were born in this universe. (Ephesians 1:3-4) God Almighty did this to uncover and reveal those daily blessings He wants to speak into your life every day, early in the morning, so you can live a blessed life. (Jeremiah 7:13, Psalm 139:16 This is a great opportunity for you to read this book of daily devotions, written under the inspiration of the Holy Spirit. (Psalm 39:3; 2 Samuel 23:2, 2 Peter 1:20-21)

Every time I hear my daughter Jennifer speak, the grace of God overflows. I strongly recommend and encourage you to read this every day early in the morning. The entrance of these words will bring light to your entire family. (Psalms 119:130)

My love, prayers, and blessings,

Harry Gomes, God's Messenger

Printed in the USA
CPSIA information can be obtained
at www.ICGtesting.com
LVHW011647240224
772712LV00065B/1716